中文写作 A Writing Guide for Learners of Chinese

中文写作 A Writing Guide for Learners of Chinese

Qin Herzberg and Larry Herzberg

with Pennylyn Dykstra-Pruim and Jennifer Redmann

Yale

UNIVERSITY PRESS

New Haven and London

Yale University Press books may be purchased in quantity for educational, business, or promotional use.
For information, please e-mail sales.press@yale.edu (U.S. office) or sales@yaleup.co.uk (U.K. office).
All illustrations in chapter 4 by Adam Wolpa.

Editors: Sarah Miller and Ashley E. Lago
Production Editor: Ann-Marie Imbornoni
Production Controller: Aldo Cupo

Set by Newgen KnowledgeWorks Pvt. Ltd., Chennai, India,
in Minion Pro, SimSun.

Printed in the United States of America.

Library of Congress Control Number: 2021931921

ISBN 978-0-300-21798-8 (paperback : alk. paper)

A catalogue record for this book is available from the British Library.

This paper meets the requirements of ANSI/NISO Z39.48-1992 (Permanence of Paper).

10 9 8 7 6 5 4 3 2 1

Contents

The Quick Overview

What is it? 中文写作 is a resource for learning to write in Chinese, designed for intermediate-level learners. In this book, you can look up how to write a specific type of text, especially those typical in learning environments in North America. You might have bought this resource on your own, for a course, or to prepare for a college credit exam. You can practice and progress through the book in sequence, but you might also use some of the models and tips right now and different topics and models later on in your Chinese learning.

What's in it? 中文写作 focuses on five types of writing typically assigned at the intermediate levels of language learning (Chapters 1–5). Each chapter presents multiple models, help with vocabulary and phrases, and tips and language notes, in order to help you practice and produce your own written texts in Chinese. You will find a range from low- to middle-intermediate (Level A) and middle- to high-intermediate (Level B) levels on the ACTFL scale. Even if you are an advanced learner, vocabulary and language tips can be helpful.

How to use this book. 中文写作 provides students with model texts as templates for crafting their own essays as homework for their Chinese classes, or for use in real-life situations, such as writing e-mails to Chinese friends. You can review and expand your vocabulary and phrases through reading or working through the text models and tips, and you can then substitute your personal information and viewpoints in creating your own texts based on the models. Level A models are intended for second-year Chinese learners at the university level; Level B models are intended for third- and fourth-year learners. High school and independent learners are encouraged to find the models and levels that best suit their needs.

For each topic, we provide basic guidelines for how to structure that kind of essay, including which types of things to include in each paragraph. You should review the specific vocabulary items in the essay and build in the vocabulary you already know or are learning in your Chinese courses in order to express your own experiences and viewpoints. The grammar patterns used in particular models should also prove useful for you as you learn to express yourself on a range of topics and through specific text genres.

The Big Idea behind the MPG Approach

中文写作 will help you learn to write in Chinese using a model-based, process-oriented, and genre-focused approach. Our catchy abbreviation for this method is MPG. With good MPG, you can get pretty far! MPG is model-based, process-oriented, and genre focused:

- Model-based: In every chapter, you will find models or examples of how to write different types of texts. You will also be guided in figuring out how to make good use of models so that you can draw on other texts you may find in the real world and use those as models. You will practice analytical reading, using vocabulary and phrases in smart ways, and sentence building.
- Process-oriented: By working through a model or set of models, you will improve your skills and build your knowledge of words, phrases, and structures that are useful in writing the type of text you are working on. Each chapter includes notes and exercises. In each section you will be guided through the writing process with prompts for which elements to include in producing that specific genre of text. The entire process (focusing on analytical reading of level-appropriate sample texts; highlighting key vocabulary and phrases; drafting, editing, and polishing a final text) is repeated in many forms and with a few twists, depending on the focus of the chapter or section.
- Genre-focused: Although improving your writing abilities in Chinese is the broad goal, you will also read carefully and build your breadth and depth of active vocabulary. We do this by focusing on specific types or genres of writing typically assigned or useful to intermediate learners. In addition to writing about yourself and describing places and things, we include writing narratives based on a set of images (Chapter 4) and e-mail and letter writing (Chapter 5) to help high school students prepare for college-credit exams and help university students with the practical tasks of telling others about their own experiences and corresponding with other Chinese speakers.

Writing in cultural context. The primary target audience and the cultural context for the writing tasks in 中文写作 is the college (or high school) language learning environment. The topics are chosen because they reflect the type of assignments typical of the intermediate levels of language learning in the North American world-language contexts while also reflecting practical writing tasks for casual and some formal types of communication with Chinese speakers, again at the intermediate levels.

More about 中文写作

During the forty years that I have taught Chinese at the college level, I have found that textbooks generally fail to provide much in the way of level-appropriate models for the various kinds of writing that I ask my students to produce and that are most useful for them in their learning journey, especially at that critical intermediate level. For example, textbooks do not provide detailed explanations concerning the format for writing a letter. Which are the customary greetings and closing? How should a letter be formatted? Rarely do textbooks include examples and focused help in producing the many essays or correspondences that we ask our students to write on different aspects of their everyday lives.

My Chinese wife and I are both longtime teachers of Chinese at Calvin University. We have discovered that students often lack an understanding of how to structure the piece of writing they are being asked to produce. They also lack sufficient vocabulary needed to write in any depth about their own personal experiences, limited as they are to the vocabulary provided in standard textbooks. In addition, a significant number of students make considerable mistakes in grammar, including the major issues of word choice and word order. This book provides models our students desperately need for all types of essays, e-mails, letters, and narrative writing at the intermediate level.

For each writing sample, we provide sections called "Words and Phrases" and "Notes." For the Level A examples, the "Words and Phrases" sections do not generally include the basic vocabulary that is taught in textbooks. Instead, we focus on building and expanding vocabulary with topic-specific words and phrases that can be added to the basic vocabulary and then adapted by learners in their own writing. Similarly, for Level B examples, we generally do not include vocabulary found in standard textbooks for middle- and high-intermediate levels. However, if words or grammatical patterns are particularly important for a text topic or genre, we include them as extra support for learners.

The useful writing samples are the base for our MPG approach to learning to write. It is our hope that learners will also use these models for additional practice in reading comprehension and text analysis. Almost all the essays are based on essays written by our college students. The intent is to provide texts that reflect the genuine life and feelings of typical students today. The "Words and Phrases" sections and models for correspondence used in this book are based on usage in mainland China rather than Taiwan or Hong Kong, where the language in such instances is much more formal and employs many more terms from classical Chinese.

Our main goal in this book is to help Chinese learners, especially at the intermediate level, to express themselves in writing in correct Chinese on common everyday topics and for common social purposes. By providing sample texts with vocabulary, tips, and strategies for success in using those texts as models, we hope to enable both learners and their teachers to enjoy the process of developing solid writing skills in Chinese.

Acknowledgments

We have enjoyed working with the masterful, intrepid, and dynamic Qin and Larry Herzberg in producing this Chinese writing guide. Their years of teaching experience and attention to detail enabled the production of the great writing models that reflect the types of texts that our students write over the course of their academic Chinese-language-learning journeys. Surrounding and supporting these models with focusing exercises and further writing guidance creates a writing guide in line with the approach of the original Yale text *Schreiben lernen: A Writing Guide for Learners of German*. 中文写作 is a perfect companion to beginning and intermediate Chinese courses, individualized learning, or as a preparation resource for placement exams. This book would not have happened without the amazing patience and diligence of Qin and Larry. We also wish to thank the Yale University Press crew, our families and friends who support us in all things, and the students who make teaching an adventure in exploration and discovery.

Pennylyn Dykstra-Pruim and Jennifer Redmann

This book would not have been possible without the invaluable contributions made by Professor Pennylyn Dykstra-Pruim of Calvin University and Professor Jennifer Redmann of Franklin and Marshall University. Professor Dykstra-Pruim and Professor Redmann provided the initial inspiration for this book through their pioneering work in model-based writing found in their writing guide for students of German entitled *Schreiben lernen*.

It was these two professors who recommended to Yale University Press that we be asked to provide a similar book for learners of the Chinese language. When we had completed our work on this book, they then reorganized it in a more easily accessible way and provided many additional writing guidelines and creative writing exercises to make the book more useful for our readers. We feel honored to have been able to partner with two such innovative foreign-language pedagogues.

We also gratefully acknowledge the delightful artwork of Adam Wolpa, who drew the wonderful cartoons used in this book.

Qin and Larry Herzberg

中文写作 A Writing Guide for Learners of Chinese

第一章 Descriptions of People 描写人 1

1.1 介绍自己和他人 Introductions—自我介绍 Myself—Level A

A

自我介绍

你好！

我的名字叫Lily Johnson，我的中文名字是张丽丽。我19岁了，我是1981年生的，我的生日是7月15号。我一米六八，55公斤。我的朋友们说我太瘦了，但是他们觉得我很漂亮。我想我没有那么好看，只是还可以。

我父亲是医生，我母亲是小学老师。我有一个哥哥和一个妹妹。我家在旧金山，但是我在华盛顿州立大学念二年级。我的专业是历史和中文。我喜欢爬山、打排球、打网球和看电影。因为我学中文，所以我想跟中国人交朋友。我希望你会成为我的朋友。

你多大了？你念大学几年级？你家在哪儿？你有没有兄弟姐妹？你的父母做什么工作？你喜欢做什么？你的生日是几月几日？请你给我回信，好不好？

祝你快乐！

丽丽

生词与短语 Words and Phrases 1.1 A

自我介绍	*zìwǒ jièshào*	self-introduction
没有那么	*méiyǒu nàme*	not so; not that
只是	*zhǐshì*	only
旧金山	*Jiùjīnshān*	San Francisco
华盛顿	*Huáshèngdùn*	Washington
州立大学	*zhōulì dàxué*	state university
专业	*zhuānyè*	major (major subject in university)
爬山	*páshān*	mountain climbing; hiking in the mountains
打排球	*dǎ páiqiú*	play volleyball
网球	*wǎngqiú*	tennis
跟. . . . . . 交朋友	*gēn . . . jiāo péngyou*	make friends with
成为	*chéngwéi*	become
回信	*huíxìn*	write back; reply (in writing)
祝你快乐	*zhù nǐ kuàilè*	wishing you joy; best wishes

1.1 Exercise 1—Vocab Grab

- Spend time reading and analyzing the model texts in the blue boxes. Use the Words and Phrases and Notes to pick up new vocabulary important for this writing topic.
- Highlight key words and phrases that you can borrow and integrate into your own text.
- Underline the pieces of information or words and phrases that you will want to change and replace with your own information.

1.1 介绍自己和他人 Introductions—自我介绍 Myself—Level B

B1

你好！

我叫张玉，是一个大三学生。我在美国的加州大学学习儿童教育。我来自中国四川的成都。我的家乡的最有名的东西是有麻辣味道的菜和举世闻名的大熊猫。我们城市有一个熊猫基地，有七、八十只大熊猫！如果你有一天会来成都，我一定会带你去看大熊猫。

我也会带你去吃成都最好吃的东西，成都有很多小吃，都非常好吃，你肯定能找到你最喜欢吃的东西。我也会带你去看成都最好玩的、最好看的地方。

我是一个独生女，爸爸是医生，妈妈是一个大学教授。你呢？你有兄弟姐妹吗？你来自哪里呢？是一个学生还是已经工作了呢？可以请你给我写信吗？我很希望我们能够成为朋友。

祝好！

你的新朋友

注 Notes

1. At the beginning of every paragraph there is an indentation, which is the space of two characters.
2. The rule used to be that there is no blank line between paragraphs. However, recently you will find that in print materials or online publications, a blank line often appears between paragraphs. In handwriting, the old rule still applies.
3. In recent decades, when date formats such as year, month, and day (called 年月日 in Chinese) are involved, Arabic numbers are used. For example, January 1, 2016, is written as 2016年1月1日. Remember, too, that when giving a date, the Chinese always give the year first, then the month and the day. Ages, telephone numbers, and street addresses should also use Arabic numbers. Hours and minutes are also increasingly written in Arabic numbers. For example, "three o'clock" could be written as 3点 or 3:00.
4. The name of the writer is indented after the valediction (complimentary close) of the letter. See Chapter 5 for details about letter writing, such as adding the date.

生词与短语 Words and Phrases 1.1 B1

大三	*dàsān*	third-year university/college student
加州	*Jiāzhōu*	California
儿童教育	*értóng jiàoyù*	elementary education
来自	*lái zì*	come from
成都	*Chéngdū*	capital city of Sichuan Province
有麻辣味道	*yǒu málà wèidào*	to be hot/spicy (food)
举世闻名	*jǔshì wénmíng*	world famous
大熊猫	*dàxióngmāo*	giant panda(s)
基地	*jīdì*	base
小吃	*xiǎochī*	snacks
肯定	*kěndìng*	definitely
独生女	*dúshēngnǚ*	only child (female)

1.1 Exercise 2—Text Analysis

- Compare texts A and B1. How are they similar and different?
- In this text you see both commas and 、(顿号 *dùnhào*). When do you use which one?

Find the answers: Notes 6 and 9 in this section.

注 Notes

5. To state distance in miles or kilometers, or the weight and height of an object, Arabic numbers are used for precision and for emphasis. Remember that both China and Taiwan use the metric system, as does almost every other country in the world except for the United States.
6. To describe someone's height, you can still use Chinese characters (一米六八). Or, to be more uniform with the other numbers mentioned in this article, you can also write 1.68米 or 168 公分 (168 centimeters).
7. The Chinese punctuation mark 、(顿号 dùnhào), which does not exist in English writing, indicates a slight pause between nouns or adjectives when they are listed or strung together.

   Examples of when 、(顿号 dùnhào) is used and not a comma:

我买了苹果、桔子和梨。 I bought apples, oranges, and pears.	我觉得我的女朋友是个很聪明的、善良的、好看的人。 I think my girlfriend is an intelligent, kind, and good-looking person.

8. Notice that right after 祝你快乐 at the end of the model text, the punctuation is not a comma but an exclamation mark. In Chinese letters, after you express good wishes at the end of letter, such as "best wishes," an exclamation mark or full stop is used, never a comma.

B2

你好！

我的名字是大卫。我今年24岁了。我希望能找到一些愿意跟我一起出去玩、旅行或者愿意带我认识一下洛杉矶的朋友们。

我刚刚搬到洛杉矶，所以我希望能更多地了解一下洛杉矶。我很喜欢去咖啡馆喝咖啡、去餐馆、看电影、参观博物馆、去公园玩。我很希望能知道哪里是这个城市里最有意思的地方、哪里是最好的购物的地点、最有特色的餐馆、最好玩的地方以及这个城市的一些有意思的历史。

我喜欢旅游、烹调、摄影、阅读、听音乐，特别是交响乐，以及自己动手做东西。我也很喜欢认识新朋友，我也非常愿意和朋友们一起做团体活动。

我会很高兴认识你！

王大卫

生词与短语 Words and Phrases 1.1 B2

愿意	*yuànyì*	be willing; wish to
或者	*huòzhě*	or (in a statement but not in a question)
洛杉矶	*Luòshānjī*	Los Angeles
了解	*liǎojiě*	to understand; find out; acquaint oneself with
咖啡馆	*kāfēiguǎn*	coffeehouse; café
参观	*cānguān*	visit (a place such as a museum or school)
购物	*gòuwù*	shopping
地点	*dìdiǎn*	location; place
特色的	*tèsède*	characteristic (adj.); distinctive; unique
以及	*yǐjí*	as well as; along with
烹调	*pēngtiáo*	cook (more formal than 做饭)
摄影	*shèyǐng*	take photos
阅读	*yuèdú*	read
特别是	*tèbiéshì*	especially
交响乐	*jiāoxiǎngyuè*	symphonic music
动手做东西	*dòngshǒu zuòdōngxi*	make things with your hands
团体活动	*tuántǐ huódòng*	group activities

1.1 Exercise 3—Vocab Grab

- Review 1.1 Exercise 1. Then, in the B1 and B2 models, highlight key phrases and underline information to be replaced when you write your own description of yourself.

1.1 Exercise 4—Text Analysis

- For each model so far, who is the audience and what is purpose of the written introduction?

注 Notes

9. When you want to say "approximately seventy to eighty giant pandas" (七十只到八十只熊猫), you can shorten it to 七、 八十只熊猫 with the Chinese punctuation mark 、(顿号 *dùnhào*) the slight-pause mark. You cannot use a comma in 七十， 八十只熊猫, because that means "seventy *and* eighty giant pandas."

10. At the end of a letter, in the last line when you wish someone well in a more formal but succinct way, use 祝好. Note that 祝好 should appear on a separate line from the body of the letter. It should, therefore, be indented by the space of two characters.

1.1 Exercise 5—A Letter of Introduction—Prewriting

Who is your audience?

Review the model texts for Levels A and B, and the Words and Phrases and Notes. Which tips for formatting and punctuation were highlighted in the model texts in this chapter?

What is your purpose?

1.1 Exercise 6—A Letter of Introduction—Text Building

Use the text builder to plan out the draft of your letter of introduction one paragraph at a time.

	Include the following:	Capture key vocab and phrases from the models in this section for these targeted items in each paragraph:
1.	• your name in English and Chinese • a physical description of yourself (age, height, weight, and other characteristics)	
2.	• facts about your family • your home town • the occupations of your parents • the number of siblings or persons in your family and their ages • your major subject in school • your career aspirations	
3.	Ask the person to whom you are writing to share some of the same sort of information about himself or herself such as age, family, major, career aspirations.	

Writing a Letter of Introduction

Step 1: Compose your letter of introduction using your key words and phrases from the text builder in 1.1 Exercise 6, as well as the sample texts as models.

Step 2: Have someone proofread your essay, highlighting phrases that they immediately recognize and understand. Double-check any items you are unsure of.

Step 3: Edit and polish your letter before handing it in for feedback, assessment, or adding to your writing portfolio.

1.2 介绍他人 Introductions—我最好的朋友 My Best Friend—Level A

A

我最好的朋友

我最好的朋友叫马克，他**是从**波士顿**来的**。马克跟我一样，也十九岁了。我们**是在**大学**认识的**。他跟我住在同一个宿舍，我们也是同班同学，因为我们都上英文课和历史课。马克很善良，也是很有趣的一个人。他对文学和历史很感兴趣。他也去过很多地方，比如说英国、法国、德国，等等，所以跟他聊天很有意思。马克也很喜欢运动。我们每个星期会在一起打网球或者游泳，也几乎会每天一块儿跑步三十分钟。

马克有两个弟弟和两个妹妹，他从小就学会了照顾弟弟妹妹，那是为什么他一点儿都不自私，总是想到别人，他真的是很善良的人，大家都喜欢他。马克的专业是国际研究，因为他对别的国家很感兴趣，也很愿意帮助别人。他希望将来到泰国或者到越南去为一个NGO工作。我想我和马克会一辈子做朋友。

生词与短语 **Words and Phrases 1.2 A**

同一个	*tóng yígè . . .*	the same . . .
同班同学	*tóngbān tóngxué*	classmate in the same class
善良	*shànliáng*	kindhearted
有趣的	*yǒuqùde*	interesting; amusing
对 . . . . . . 感兴趣	*duì . . . gǎnxìngqù*	be interested in . . .
比如说	*bǐrú shuō*	for example
等等	*děngděng*	etc.
聊天	*liáotiān*	chat
几乎	*jīhū*	almost
学会	*xuéhuì*	successfully learn how to do something
照顾	*zhàogù*	take care of
自私	*zìsī*	selfish
国际	*guójì*	international
泰国	*Tàiguó*	Thailand
一辈子	*yíbèizi*	all one's life; for a lifetime
做朋友	*zuò péngyou*	be friends

注 Notes

1. Notice that the title of an article or essay in Chinese should be placed in the center of the page above the first line of the body of the text, not on the left side of the first line. In other words, titles should be centered and not left-aligned. Between the title and the body of the article or essay there should be two blank lines.

注 Notes

2. The 是 . . . 的 pattern is used to emphasize details about past events, including when, where, how, and with whom something happened, but it does not include what happened.

是从 . . . . . . 来的 came from . . . ; is from . . .

例 句 Example Sentences

她**是从**纽约**来的**。
Tā shì cóng Niǔyuē láide.
She's from New York.

李小文**是从**中国**来的**。
Lǐ Xiǎowén shì cóng Zhōngguó láide.
Li Xiaowen is from China.

是在 . . . . . . 认识的 met in . . .

例 句 Example Sentences

我们**是在**大学**认识的**。
Wǒmen shì zài dàxué rènshide.
We met in college.

小张和小李**是在**咖啡店**认识的**。
Xiǎo Zhāng hé Xiǎo Lǐ shì zài kāfēidiàn rènshide.
Little Zhang and Little Li met in a coffeehouse.

1.2 Exercise 1—Writing Tips—Level A

- Read the model text closely, paying attention to the highlighted words.
- Note the words or phrases that you will want to change to appropriately describe a best friend of yours. Start your list of new target words for this writing assignment in the blue box. Ask a partner or tutor to check your word choices.
- Using the model text as your base and substituting your target new words for this topic, you are ready to draft your essay.

1.2 介绍他人 Introductions—我最好的朋友 My Best Friend—Level B

生词与短语 **Words and Phrases 1.2 B**

安娜	*Ānnà*	Anna
第一代	*dìyīdài*	first generation
混血儿	*hùnxuè-ér*	person of mixed race
奥林匹克比赛	*Aòlínpǐkè bǐsài*	Olympic competition; olympiad
曾经	*céngjīng*	previously; formerly
专业的	*zhuānyède*	professional
体操运动员	*tǐcāo yùndòngyuán*	gymnast
滑冰	*huábīng*	ice skate
队	*duì*	team
训练	*xùnliàn*	drill; practice; training
吃素	*chīsù*	be a vegetarian
兔子	*tùzi*	rabbit
坚果	*jiānguǒ*	nut(s)
不碰	*búpèng*	to not touch
垃圾食品	*lājī shípǐn*	junk food
不过	*búguò*	but; however
苗条	*miáotiáo*	slender
举办	*jǔbàn*	conduct; put on
演讲比赛	*yǎnjiǎng bǐsài*	speech competition(s)
合唱团	*héchàngtuán*	chorus
文艺演出	*wényì yǎnchū*	theatrical performance(s)
热心	*rèxīn*	enthusiastic; passionate
联合国	*Liánhéguó*	United Nations
人道主义	*réndàozhǔyì*	humanitarian
援助团体	*yuánzhù tuántǐ*	aid organization(s)
全世界	*quán shìjiè*	the entire world
救济	*jiùjì*	relieve; relief

B

我最好的朋友

我最好的朋友叫安娜，她的爸爸是德国人，妈妈是中国人，所以安娜是她家的第一代美国人。

安娜是一个混血儿，有黑色的头发，圆圆的大眼睛，高高瘦瘦的，非常漂亮。她也非常聪明，她上中学的时候就参加了很多次数学奥林匹克比赛。

安娜的妈妈曾经是一位专业的体操运动员，她的爸爸是一个滑冰运动员，所以安娜对体育活动很感兴趣。我和安娜就是**在**学校的游泳队训练**时**认识的。现在我们**除了**每周在一起游泳**以外**，也一起跑步、打篮球，冬天的时候我们还会一起滑冰。

安娜从上大学就开始吃素，我常常开玩笑说看她吃饭就像看一只兔子吃饭一样，因为她只吃蔬菜、水果、坚果这些很健康的食品，从来不碰垃圾食品，不过，她真的很健康，从来不生病，也非常苗条。

安娜和我也很喜欢参加学校举办的各种学生活动，比如我们都参加了学校的学生演讲比赛、合唱团的文艺演出。

安娜也非常热心帮助别人。每年夏天，她都会参加联合国的人道主义援助团体，到全世界各地去帮助穷人和需要救济的人们。她真是一个非常善良的人。

注 **Notes**

3. **在** . . . . . . **时** is a more elegant way than . . . 的时候 for saying "when"

   例句 **Example Sentences**

   我爸爸妈妈是**在**大学念书**时**认识的。
   Wǒ bàba māma shì zài dàxué niànshū shí rènshide.
   My parents met when they were students in college.

   爸爸**在**美国出差**时**每天给我打电话。
   Bàba zài Měiguó chūchāi shí měitiān gěi wǒ dǎ diànhuà.
   When Dad's in America on a business trip, he calls me every day.

4. **除了** . . . . . . **以外** *chúle . . . yǐwài* means "besides/in addition to"

   例句 **Example Sentences**

   我**除了**学汉语**以外**，也学日语。
   Wǒ chúle xué Hànyǔ yǐwài, yě xué Rìyǔ.
   In addition to studying Chinese, I'm also studying Japanese.
   (This can also be translated as "I'm also studying Japanese in addition to Chinese." However, in Chinese the expression 除了 . . . 以外 always comes in the first clause of the sentence and never in the second clause, as is possible in English.)

   小林**除了**会唱歌**以外**，也会跳舞。
   Xiǎo Lín chúle huì chànggē yǐwài, yě huì tiàowǔ.
   Besides knowing how to sing, Little Lin can also dance.

1.2 Exercise 2—Text Analysis

Compare the "My Best Friend" models for Level A and Level B. Can you identify elements or words in the Level B models that indicate a more advanced level of language?

1.2 Exercise 3—A Matter of Degree: Modifying Adjectives

Practice reading and writing these adverbs and adjective phrases.

Modifiers/Adverbs			Practice Writing	例子 Examples—Practice Reading		
非常	*fēicháng*	extremely; unusually; extraordinarily		非常高	*fēicháng gāo*	extremely tall
特别	*tèbié*	especially; particularly		特别高	*tèbié gāo*	especially tall
极了	*jíle*	extremely		高极了	*gāojíle*	extremely tall
真	*zhēn*	really; truly		真高	*zhēn gāo*	really tall
很	*hěn*	very		很高	*hěn gāo*	very tall
相当	xiāngdāng	quite; fairly		相当高	*xiāngdāng gāo*	quite tall; fairly tall
比较	*bǐjiào*	relatively; comparatively; rather		比较高	*bǐjiào gāo*	rather tall
有一点	*yǒu yìdiǎn*	a little		有一点高	*yǒu yìdiǎn gāo*	a little tall
不太	*bútài*	not too		不太高	*bútài gāo*	not too tall
不	*bù*	not		不高	*bùgāo*	not tall
太	*tài*	too		太高	*tài gāo*	too tall

1.2 Exercise 4—Modifying Adjectives

Express these adjective phrases in Chinese.

1. fairly slender
2. very amusing
3. not too intelligent
4. not good-looking
5. especially kind
6. relatively old

1.2 Exercise 5—Describing Your Best Friend—Drafting

Review the vocabulary and phrases you need as you plan each paragraph of your essay. Read through the models again and note key vocabulary for each paragraph in the blue spaces below.

Paragraph 1: Tell the reader your best friend's name, age, hometown, a bit about his/her family, and where you met.

Paragraph 2: Describe your friend's physical appearance and his/her personality, including why you are so fond of your friend.

Paragraph 3: Describe your friend's interests, hobbies, and special talents.

Paragraph 4: Give your friend's major in school and his/her future career goals. Conclude with a remark about your hope for your friend and for the future of your relationship.

Describing Your Best Friend—Level B

Following the model and using your vocabulary and phrases from above, draft your essay one paragraph at a time.

1.3 介绍自己的家庭 Introductions—我的家庭 My Family—Level A

生词与短语 Words and Phrases 1.3 A

口	*kǒu*	measure word for people in a family
壮	*zhuàng*	strong
褐色	*hèsè*	brown
戴眼镜	*dài yǎnjìng*	wear glasses
志愿工作	*zhìyuàn gōngzuò*	volunteer work
跟人交往	*gēn rén jiāowǎng*	interact with people
充满	*chōngmǎn*	full of; brimming with
智慧	*zhìhuì*	wisdom; intelligence
特别	*tèbié*	especially
具有	*jùyǒu*	possess
同情心	*tóngqíngxīn*	sympathy
稍微……一点	*shāowēi . . . yìdiǎn*	slightly; a bit
卷发	*juǎnfà*	curly hair
上脸书	*shàng liǎnshū*	get on Facebook
首饰	*shǒushi*	jewelry
勤奋	*qínfèn*	diligent
粉刺	*fěncì*	acne
弹钢琴	*tán gāngqín*	play the piano
幽默感	*yōumògǎn*	sense of humor
网上	*wǎngshàng*	on the internet
视频网站	*shìpín wǎngzhàn*	video websites such as YouTube
密切	*mìqiè*	close; intimate
想念	*xiǎngniàn*	miss; long to see again
盼望	*pànwàng*	hope for; long for
到来	*dàolái*	arrive; come

A

我爱我的家人

我家有四口人：爸爸、妈妈、我和弟弟。

我的爸爸52岁了，他是一个高中的数学老师。他很高很壮，有蓝色的眼睛，深褐色的头发，戴眼镜。我的爸爸很喜欢做志愿工作、跟人交往。我很爱我的爸爸，因为他充满了智慧而且特别具有同情心。

我的妈妈45岁了，她是一个律师。她**比**我**稍微**矮**一点**，有蓝色的眼睛和金色的卷发。她很爱唱歌，如果她有时间的话，她很喜欢上脸书和自己做首饰。我爱我的妈妈，因为她工作得很勤奋。

我的弟弟15岁了，但是他比我高多了，他上高二，他也有蓝色的眼睛和金色的卷发，他的脸上也有很多粉刺。弟弟学弹钢琴已经11年了，所以他弹得非常好。他也很有幽默感。我很爱我的弟弟，我们经常一起看网上的视频网站。

我的家庭虽然很小，但是我们的关系很密切。

我爱我的家人，我非常想念他们，我盼望圣诞节快点到来，那样我就能回家去看他们！

1.3介绍自己的家庭 Introductions—我的家庭 My Family—Level B

注 Notes

1. You can use the following phrase for making a comparison in Chinese.

比	+	[noun]	稍微	+	[adjective]	一点
bǐ		______	*shāowēi*		________	*yìdiǎn*

比 indicates a ratio or comparison. This phrase translates to: slightly more adjective than noun.

Examples

比我稍微矮一点

slightly shorter than I

比我稍微高一点

slightly taller than I

比我稍微苗条一点

slightly more slender than I

比我稍微胖一点

slightly fatter than I

B

我的家庭

我家有四口人：爸爸、妈妈、我和妹妹。

我的妈妈44岁了，她是在印度出生和长大的。她16岁的时候来纽约上大学，在那里，她认识了在纽约出生和长大的爸爸。

我妈妈是一个心理学家。很多人都认为她一定是一个非常有耐心的人，但是其实我妈妈很没有耐心。她总是开玩笑说"我的耐心都花在我的病人的身上了"。我妈妈没有什么特别的爱好，这让我很高兴，因为这让她有更多的时间带我去买东西。

我爸爸50岁了。他是一个工程师。他的性格和我妈妈正相反。我的妈妈在周末时常常坐在家里看书。我从来没看到过我爸爸坐下来读一本书。他喜欢做冒险的事情，特别是高空冒险。他高中毕业时做了跳伞运动，他40岁生日时玩了悬挂式滑翔机。我的妈妈非常怕高，她连坐过山车都会吓得大喊大叫。

我的妹妹16岁了。她10个月大的时候我的爸爸妈妈从印度领养了她。她在学校的行进乐队里演奏小号。她最喜欢的学科是数学。她像我爸爸一样，很不喜欢阅读；但她也像我妈妈，她一样怕高。

生词与短语 Words and Phrases 1.3 B

印度	*Yìndù*	India
纽约	*Niǔyuē*	New York
心理学家	*xīnlǐxuéjiā*	psychologist
耐心	*nàixīn*	patient
其实	*qíshí*	actually
花在……身上	*huā zài . . . shēnshang*	expend/use up on (somebody)
特别	*tèbié*	special
正相反	*zhèng xiāngfǎn*	just the opposite
冒险	*màoxiǎn*	risky; dangerous
特别是	*tèbiéshì*	especially
高空	*gāokōng*	high altitude
跳伞	*tiàosǎn*	parachute
悬挂式滑翔机	*xuán guà shì huá xiáng jī*	hang-gliding
过山车	*guòshānchē*	roller coaster
吓	*xià*	scare; frighten
大喊大叫	*dàhǎn dàjiào*	shout at the top of one's voice
领养	*lǐngyǎng*	adopt
行进乐队	*xíngjìn yùeduì*	marching band
演奏	*yǎnzòu*	perform (on a musical instrument)
小号	*xiǎohào*	trumpet
学科	*xuékē*	subject in school
阅读	*yuèdú*	read

注 Notes

2.

爷爷	*yéye*	paternal grandfather
奶奶	*nǎinai*	paternal grandmother
外公	*wàigōng*	maternal grandfather (southern China)
外婆	*wàipó*	maternal grandmother (southern China)
姥爷	*lǎoye*	maternal grandfather (northern China)
姥姥	*lǎolao*	maternal grandmother (northern China)

3. 父 | 母

父母离婚了	*fùmǔ líhūn le*	parents got divorced
父亲再婚了	*fùqin zàihūn le*	father remarried
母亲再婚了	*mǔqin zàihūn le*	mother remarried
父亲去世了	*fùqin qùshì le*	father is deceased
母亲去世了	*mǔqin qùshì le*	mother is deceased
亡父	*wángfù*	deceased father
亡母	*wángmǔ*	deceased mother
继父	*jìfù*	stepfather
继母	*jìmǔ*	stepmother
养父养母	*yǎngfù yǎngmǔ*	adoptive parents

4. 哥哥 | 姐姐 | 弟弟 | 妹妹

同父异母的哥哥/弟弟/姐姐/妹妹
tóngfù yìmǔ de gēge/dìdi/jiějie/mèimei
older half brother/younger half brother/older half sister/younger half sister from the same father but different mother

同母异父的哥哥/弟弟/姐姐/妹妹
tóngmǔ yìfù de gēge/dìdi/jiějie/mèimei
from the same mother but different father

5. 常用的家庭成员的称呼 **Common terms related to family members.** 一对双胞胎 *yíduì shuāngbāotāi* means a pair of twins (in written form, 孪生 *luánshēng* is often used).

1.3 Exercise—Writing about Your Family—Drafting
Review the vocabulary words and phrases you need as you plan each paragraph of your essay. Read through the models again and note key vocabulary words for each paragraph in the blue spaces below.

Paragraph 1: Begin with the number of members of your family, including siblings. Then give detailed information about a parent. Including age, physical appearance, occupation, and hobbies and interests. Conclude by describing your parent's personality.

Paragraph 2: Give some detailed information about another parent or grandparent.

Paragraph 3: Provide some information about siblings or other persons in your family. If they are still students, give their year in school. If they have career ambitions, mention those.

Paragraph 4: Conclude with your feelings about your family, including what you most enjoy about being a member of your family.

注 Notes

6. There are no terms in Chinese for stepbrothers and stepsisters (who have no parent in common). You may simply refer to them the same way you would if they were your siblings by blood, that is, as 哥哥，姐姐，弟弟，妹妹.

Writing about Your Family—Level B
Using the models and your vocabulary words and phrases, draft your essay one paragraph at a time.

1.4 名人 About Celebrities—我最喜欢的电影演员 My Favorite Movie Star—Level A

Figure 1.4.1 Scarlett Johansson
(Photo credit: Dick Thomas Johnson)

A

我最喜欢的电影演员

我最喜欢的电影明星是Scarlett Johansson。 我觉得她不但是非常好的演员，也是最漂亮的女演员。她是1984年在纽约市出生的，5尺3寸高，有一点矮，但很苗条。

她的电影我差不多都看过。有的是很严肃的电影，像The Girl with the Pearl Earring、The Prestige 和 The Other Boleyn Girl。可是她最近演的电影都很有娱乐性，像The Avengers、Captain America 和 Her。无论是什么电影，Scarlett 总是演得很好，好像她真的就是那个角色。因为我喜欢她演的那些人物，所以我更喜欢她。除了演电影以外，她也会唱歌，已经出了两个专辑。Scarlett Johansson 和她的弟弟 Hunter 是双胞胎。她也有一个哥哥和一个姐姐。2014年她跟一个法国人结婚了，同年，她生了一个女儿。

生词与短语 Words and Phrases 1.4 A

演员	*yǎnyuán*	actor/actress
明星	*míngxīng*	star
严肃	*yánsù*	serious
演	*yǎn*	perform/act
娱乐性	*yúlèxìng*	an entertaining or amusing nature
无论	*wúlùn*	no matter; regardless of
角色	*juésè* (commonly mispronounced as *jiǎosè*)	person; figure; character (in a work of art)
专辑	*zhuānjí*	album
双胞胎	*shuāngbāotāi*	twins
跟……结婚	*gēn . . . jiéhūn*	marry
同年	*tóngnián*	same year

1.5 名人 About Celebrities—我最喜欢的歌手 My Favorite Singer—Level B

Figure 1.5.1 Taylor Swift
(Photo credit: Ronald Woan)

1.5 Exercise 1—音乐风格 Styles of Music

What kind of music do you enjoy? Check all that apply.

_____	流行音乐	*liúxíng yīnyuè*	popular music
_____	乡村音乐	*xiāngcūn yīnyuè*	country and western music
_____	摇滚音乐	*yáogǔn yīnyuè*	rock music
_____	爵士音乐	*juéshì yīnyuè*	jazz music
_____	嘻哈音乐	*xīhā yīnyuè*	hip-hop music
_____	说唱	*shuōchàng*	rap music
_____	古典音乐	*gǔdiǎn yīnyuè*	classical music

Discuss with a partner your favorite musicians and why you like them.

B

我最喜欢的歌手

我最喜欢的流行音乐的歌手是Taylor Swift。在过去的十年里，Taylor Swift已经出了五部音乐专辑。她的第一部专辑是乡村音乐，可是最近几年，她的音乐风格转向流行音乐。Taylor的歌曲都是她自己作词、自己谱曲的。Taylor Swift的许多歌曲都得到了很多年轻女子的认同，那也是我喜欢她的歌曲的原因。她的歌曲的特点是题材十分广泛，比如说：上学的第一天、恋爱关系的破裂，等等。Taylor的歌词往往是坦率、真诚地流露出她的真实感情。

很难说哪一首Taylor的歌曲或者专辑是我最喜爱的，因为她的每一部专辑都不同，却都令人愉快。在过去的十年里，Taylor Swift已经成为国际超级明星，而她的音乐已经感动了成千上万的年轻女子的心。

生词与短语 Words and Phrases 1.5 B

歌手	*gēshǒu*	singer
流行音乐	*liúxíng yīnyuè*	popular music
过去	*guòqù*	the past
部	*bù*	measure word for movies, albums, etc.
专辑	*zhuānjí*	album
乡村音乐	*xiāngcūn yīnyuè*	country and western music
风格	*fēng-gé*	style
转向	*zhuǎnxiàng*	turn toward
歌曲	*gēqǔ*	songs
作词	*zuòcí*	compose the lyrics
谱曲	*pǔqǔ*	compose a piece of music
许多	*xǔduō*	more elegant way of saying 很多
得到……认同	*dédào . . . rèntóng*	get (somebody) to identify with
女子	*nǚzǐ*	woman
原因	*yuányīn*	reason
特点	*tèdiǎn*	special characteristic; trait
题材	*tícái*	topic; subject; theme
广泛	*guǎngfàn*	extensive; wide-ranging; broad
恋爱	*liàn-ài*	(romantic) love
破裂	*pòliè*	breakup
歌词	*gēcí*	lyrics
往往	*wǎngwǎng*	often; frequently
坦率	*tǎnshuài*	frank; candid
真诚地	*zhēnchéngde*	sincerely; genuinely
流露出	*liúlùchū*	show; reveal
感情	*gǎnqíng*	feelings
首	*shǒu*	measure word for songs, poems, etc.
不同	*bùtóng*	not the same
令人愉快	*lìngrén yúkuài*	make people happy
超级明星	*chāojí míngxīng*	superstar
感动	*gǎndòng*	move; affect

注 Notes

When foreign names are translated into Chinese, often only the last name is used. For example, President John F. Kennedy was simply referred to as 肯尼迪总统（*Kěnnídí Zǒngtǒng*, or President Kennedy). But when his full name is mentioned, then it must be written as 约翰. F. 肯尼迪. In other words, a dot is always placed between the first name and middle initial and last name, with a space between each.

1.5 Exercise 2—我最喜欢的名人 My Favorite Celebrities

Review the list of types of celebrities. Give examples of your favorite celebrities in at least three categories, writing their names in Chinese.

歌手	*gēshǒu*	singer
演员	*yǎnyuán*	actor/actress
运动员	*yùndòngyuán*	athlete
作家	*zuòjiā*	writer
政治家	*zhèngzhìjiā*	politician
电影制片人	*diànyǐng zhìpiàn rén*	filmmaker
厨师	*chúshī*	chef
企业家	*qǐyèjiā*	entrepreneur

1.6 名人 About Celebrities—我最喜欢的运动员 My Favorite Athlete—Level B

注 Notes

1. When writing anything in Chinese, the words on both the right and the left margins should line up, even if this means breaking up a character compound. Look for a compound in the essay on the right that is split in this way. This is very different from writing in English, where the priority is not to split a word in the middle but to place it at the beginning of the next line.
2. Although the terms 女子, 女人, and 妇女 (*fùnǚ*) all mean "women," they carry different connotations. 妇女 is the most formal term. However, when talking about sports, the less formal term 女子 is used to distinguish women athletes from male athletes. 女人 traditionally has a derogatory connotation and was used by men when making disparaging comments about the behavior of women. However, women may choose to use it for themselves without any of the derogatory connotation that men have added to that term.

B

我最喜欢的运动员

我最喜欢的运动员是加拿大人Sidney Crosby。他是匹兹堡的企鹅冰球队的队长。因为匹兹堡的企鹅冰球队一直是我支持的冰球队，而他是那个冰球队的队长，所以他当然也就成为我最喜爱的球员。

无论跟谁比，Crosby都是世界上最好的冰球运动员。他身高5英尺11寸，体重215磅。他最好的技巧是他有非常好的冰上滑行技术。他也具有能看出对手将要做什么的本领，所以**只要**有他出场，企鹅队**就**能进球。他能帮助他的同队的队员发挥出最好的水平。他的绰号是"Sid the Kid"，因为他们赢得冰球比赛的最高奖—斯坦利杯的时候，他才21岁。

Crosby也很热心回馈社会，他经常到匹兹堡的医院去看望住院儿童，给他们带来惊喜。因为冰球运动需要很贵的器材，他成立了一个基金会捐款给当地的儿童买冰球器材。他认为每一个孩子都应该有打冰球的机会。

Crosby是我最喜欢的冰球运动员**不但**是因为他的出众的冰球技巧，**而且**是因为他有非常好的品质和善良助人的本性。

生词与短语 **Words and Phrases 1.6 B**

匹兹堡	*Pǐzībǎo*	Pittsburgh
企鹅	*qǐ-é*	penguins
冰球队	*bīngqiúduì*	hockey team
队长	*duìzhǎng*	team captain
支持	*zhīchí*	support; root for
喜爱	*xǐ-ài*	to love; be fond of
无论跟谁比	*wúlùn gēn shéi bǐ*	no matter compared to whom
技巧	*jìqiǎo*	technique; skill
滑行技术	*huáxíng jìshù*	skating skill
具有	*jùyǒu*	possess
对手	*duìshǒu*	opponent
将要	*jiāngyào*	is about to . . .
本领	*běnlǐng*	ability
出场	*chūchǎng*	take the field; appear on the scene
进球	*jìnqiú*	score (a goal)
发挥出	*fāhuīchū*	bring into play; bring forth
水平	*shuǐpíng*	level
绰号	*chuòhào*	nickname
赢得	*yíngdé*	win; gain
奖	*jiǎng*	prize
斯坦利杯	*Sītǎnlì bēi*	Stanley Cup
热心	*rèxīn*	enthusiastic; passionate
回馈	*huíkuì*	give back (in the abstract sense)
看望	*kànwàng*	visit; look in on
住院	*zhù yuàn*	be hospitalized
惊喜	*jīngxǐ*	unexpected joy
器材	*qìcái*	equipment
成立	*chénglì*	to establish; set up
基金会	*jījīnhuì*	(charitable) foundation
捐款	*juānkuǎn*	donate money
当地	*dāngdì*	local
出众	*chūzhòng*	outstanding; out of the ordinary
品质	*pǐnzhì*	nature; character
善良	*shànliáng*	kindhearted
助人	*zhùrén*	help people
本性	*běnxìng*	character; disposition

Figure 1.6.1 Sidney Crosby
(Photo credit: Wikimedia Commons)

注 Notes

These two-part constructions were featured in the preceding model texts:

只要……**就**…… *zhǐ yào . . . jiù* as long as

1. **只要**有小林来，聚会**就**会很热闹。
Zhǐ yào yǒu Xiǎo Lín lái, jùhuì jiù huì hěn rènào.
As long as Little Lin comes, the party (gathering) will be very lively/fun.

2. **只要**我们继续努力地打，我们**就**一定会赢！
Zhǐ yào wǒmen jìxù nǔlìde dǎ, wǒmen jiù yídìng huì yíng!
As long as we keep playing hard, we'll definitely win!

不但……**而且**…… *búdàn . . . érqiě* not only . . . but also

1. 安迪**不但**会说汉语，**而且**会写汉字。
Āndí búdàn huì shuō Hànyǔ, érqiě huì xiě Hànzì.
Andy not only can speak Chinese but can also write Chinese characters.

2. 小林**不但**长得漂亮，**而且**非常聪明。
Xiǎo Lín búdàn zhǎngde piàoliàng, érqiě fēicháng cōngmíng.
Little Lin is not only pretty but also extremely smart.

1.6 Exercise 1—Sentence Completion

Use the constructions above to complete the sentences.

________________________________, 我就会每天学习。(I will study every day.)

________________________________, 我们就会玩得开心。(We will have fun.)

我不但喜欢看电影 (I not only enjoy going to the movies), ________________________________。

我们不但打曲棍球 (We not only play hockey), ________________________________。

1.6 Exercise 2—Preparing to Write about Your Favorite Celebrity

Choose a celebrity and do research to gather some relevant facts. Make notes below.

年龄	**Age**
外貌 (*wàimào*)	**Appearance**
出生地	**Birthplace**
家庭	**Family**
成就	**Achievements**

1.6 Exercise 3—Drafting an Essay about Your Favorite Celebrity

Use your notes to begin drafting an essay that follows this structure. Note down key vocabulary items you will use in each box.

Paragraph 1: Give the name and type of career of your favorite celebrity, followed by a physical description that includes his or her age.

Paragraph 2: Mention the major achievements of your favorite celebrity.

Paragraph 3: Describe why you admire this celebrity and why you think he or she is so special.

Writing about Your Favorite Celebrity
Drawing on your notes, write your essay one paragraph at a time. Edit, polish, and proofread your essay before handing it in for feedback or assessment, or adding to your writing portfolio.

1.7 理想的伴侣 Ideal Partners—理想的男朋友 My Ideal Boyfriend—Level A

注 Notes

1. This section introduces models to write about an ideal 伴侣 *bànlǚ* boyfriend or girlfriend and an ideal 爱人 *àirén* spouse. Note that 爱人 is only used to mean "spouse" in mainland China. In Taiwan, Hong Kong, and elsewhere this term means "lover" when used outside of marriage. Some of the descriptions in the models can be used to describe either male or female partners, but of course many are gender specific.

生词与短语 **Words and Phrases 1.7 A**

理想	*lǐxiǎng*	ideal
必须	*bìxū*	must; have to
开朗	*kāilǎng*	open; optimistic
幽默感	*yōumògǎn*	sense of humor
跟……相处	*gēn . . . xiāngchǔ*	interact with somebody
抱怨	*bàoyuàn*	complain
倾听	*qīngtīng*	listen attentively
认真	*rènzhēn*	conscientious; earnest
感觉	*gǎnjué*	feelings
脾气	*píqi*	temperament; disposition
吵架	*chǎojià*	quarrel
让着	*ràngzhe*	yield; give in
发脾气	*fā píqi*	lose one's temper; get angry
想法	*xiǎngfǎ*	opinion; way of thinking
独立	*dúlì*	independent
勇敢	*yǒng-gǎn*	brave; courageous
感到	*gǎndào*	feel (an emotion)
安全	*ānquán*	safe
保护	*bǎohù*	protect

A

理想的男朋友

我的理想的男朋友必须是一个开朗的人，有幽默感，而且不但能跟我相处得好，也能跟别人相处得很好。我的男朋友应该很英俊，高高的、瘦瘦的，最好有黑色的头发、蓝色的眼睛、高高的鼻子。

他也应该很喜欢体育运动，因为我自己很喜欢跑步、打篮球和游泳，如果他也喜欢这些体育活动，我们就可以经常在一起做运动。

我常常听到我的其他的女朋友们抱怨说她们的男朋友不倾听她们的话，所以我希望我的男朋友会认真地倾听我的感觉。

他也应该是一个脾气很好的人，**如果**我们吵架**的话**，他应该让着我一点儿，等我发完了脾气，再慢慢地告诉我他的想法。

虽然我觉得我很独立、勇敢，但是我还是希望当我跟我的男朋友在一起的时候，他会让我感到安全，让我感到他会保护我。

注 Notes

2. **如果……的话** *rúguŏ . . . de huà* if

Although 如果 by itself means "if," the Chinese will often bookend the "if" clause with 如果 at the beginning and with 的话 at the end for emphasis. 例句 Example Sentences:

如果你周末有时间**的话**，请来我家参加聚会。
Rúguŏ nĭ zhōumò yŏu shíjiān de huà, qĭng lái wŏ jiā cānjiā jùhuì.
If you're free on the weekend, please come to my house for a party.

如果你需要帮助**的话**，请给我打电话。
Rúguŏ nĭ xūyào bāngzhù de huà, qĭng gĕi wŏ dă diànhuà.
If you need help, please call me.

1.7 Exercise 1—Reading Practice—阅读练习

1. 特点 *tèdiăn* special characteristic/trait
那个人的特点是非常热情直爽。*Nèige rén de tèdiăn shì fēicháng rèqíng zhíshuăng* (candid).
2. 跟……结婚 *gēn . . . jiéhūn* marry
如果你真心地爱一个人，你就应该跟他/她结婚。*Rúguŏ nĭ zhēnxīn de ài yíge rén, nĭ jiù yīnggāi gēn tā jiéhūn.*
3. 恋爱 *liàn-ài* (romantic) love
恋爱是许多流行歌曲的主题。*Liàn-ài shì xŭduō liúxíng gēqŭ de zhŭtí.*
4. 感情 *gănqíng* feelings
虽然他离开家乡很久了，但他还是对家乡的人和事有很深厚的感情。*Suírán tā líkāi jiāxiāng hĕn jiŭ le, dàn tā háishi duì jiāxiāng de rén hé shì yŏu hĕn shēnhòu* (deep) *de gănqíng.*
5. 喜爱 *xĭ-ài* to love; be fond of
我们都非常喜爱体育活动。*Wŏmen dōu fēicháng xiài tĭyù huódòng.*
6. 品质 *pĭnzhì* character; quality
他有优良的道德品质，所以人人都敬佩他。*Tā yŏu yōuliáng* (excellent) *de dàodé pĭnzhì, suóyĭ rénrén dōu jìngpèi* (admire) *tā.*
7. 本性 *bĕnxìng* nature; natural disposition
那个人的本性很善良。*Nàge rén de bĕnxìng hĕn shànliáng.*

1.7 Exercise 2—Vocabulary, Adjectives

How important is this characteristic in an ideal partner?
当你选择理想的伴侣时，以下哪些特点对你来说是最重要的？

	Not important				Very important
开朗	1	2	3	4	5
幽默感	1	2	3	4	5
善良	1	2	3	4	5
苗条	1	2	3	4	5
高	1	2	3	4	5
独立	1	2	3	4	5
会唱歌	1	2	3	4	5
有趣	1	2	3	4	5
热心	1	2	3	4	5
吃素	1	2	3	4	5

1.7 Exercise 1—Answers

1. That person's special traits are exuberance and frankness.
2. If you wholeheartedly love a person, you ought to marry him/her.
3. Love is the main theme of a great many popular songs.
4. Although he left his hometown a long time ago, he still has deep feelings for the people and things there.
5. We are all really fond of (love) athletic activities.
6. He has an excellent moral character, so everyone admires him.
7. That person is kind by nature.

1.8 理想的伴侣 Ideal Partners—我的理想的爱人 My Ideal Wife—Level A

我的理想的爱人

A

我理想的爱人应当是一个又善良又温柔的人。当然，我希望她比较漂亮，但是最重要的是她应当是个好人，不但对我好也对别人好。

我也希望我的对象是一个很有趣的人，像我一样喜欢开玩笑，所以我们在一起时会玩儿得很开心。因为我很喜欢旅游，所以希望她也喜欢旅游，那样我们就可以一块儿到各地去看看。我也很喜欢看球赛和电影，所以希望她也喜欢做那些事情。

我自己不会做饭，所以如果她会做饭而且做得好就太好了。但是如果我能遇见一个善良温柔的好人，而且我爱她，她也爱我，她会不会做饭、会不会喜欢我喜欢做的事情、她高不高、瘦不瘦就都没有关系，我就会跟她结婚。

生词与短语 Words and Phrases 1.8 A

理想	*lǐxiǎng*	ideal
爱人	*àirén*	spouse
善良	*shànliáng*	kindhearted
温柔	*wēnróu*	gentle
比较	*bǐjiào*	relatively; comparatively; fairly
对……好	*duì . . . hǎo*	be good to somebody; be good for somebody
对象	*duìxiàng*	romantic partner
有趣的	*yǒuqùde*	interesting; fun
像……一样	*xiàng . . . yíyàng*	just like . . .
开玩笑	*kāi wánxiào*	to joke
时	*shí*	shortened form for 时候 used in writing an article or letter
玩儿得很开心	*wánr de hěn kāixīn*	have a good time
球赛	*qiúsài*	ball game
遇见	*yùjiàn*	meet; come across
没有关系	*méiyǒu guānxi*	it doesn't matter
跟……结婚	*gēn . . . jiéhūn*	marry (somebody)

1.8 Exercise—Vocab Grab

Review the models presented in this chapter and grab some phrases that you might use to talk about an ideal mate. Collect them here and practice writing them. You can compare your list with those of others.

1.9 理想的伴侣 Ideal Partners—理想的女朋友 My Ideal Girlfriend—Level B

生词与短语 Words and Phrases 1.9 B

理想	*lǐxiǎng*	ideal
性格	*xìng-gé*	personality
无聊	*wúliáo*	boring
脾气	*píqi*	temperament; disposition
跟……打交道	*gēn . . . dǎ jiāodào*	have dealings with
温柔	*wēnróu*	gentle
愿望	*yuànwàng*	hopes; aspirations
在兴趣上	*zài xìngqù shàng*	in terms of interests
尝试	*chángshì*	attempt; try
努力	*nǔlì*	make a great effort; try hard
真诚	*zhēnchéng*	sincere; genuine
善良	*shànliáng*	kindhearted
讨厌	*tǎoyàn*	loathe; detest
虚假	*xūjiǎ*	false; sham

B

理想的女朋友

我的理想的女朋友需要有很开朗的性格，我觉得性格不开朗的人很无聊。

她也需要有好脾气，我不喜欢跟一个常常会生气的人打交道，我当然希望她很温柔。

她也应该很漂亮。我觉得男人都会有这个愿望，哪个男人说他不喜欢漂亮的女孩就没有说真话。

在兴趣上，如果她的跟我的不一样没有关系，因为我很喜欢尝试新的东西，所以如果她和我有很不一样的兴趣的话，我就会努力地学习她喜欢做的事情。

最后，她必须是一个真诚善良的人，我很讨厌虚假而又不愿意助人的人。

1.9 Exercise—Grammar Patterns

These phrases appear throughout this chapter. How many can you recall?

对……感兴趣	*duì . . gǎnxìngqù*
像……一样	*xiàng . . . yíyàng*
不但……而且……	*búdàn . . . érqiě . . .*
除了……以外	*chúle . . . yǐwài*
跟……交朋友	*gēn . . .jiāo péngyou*
只要……就……	*zhǐ yào . . . jiù . . .*
如果……的话	*rúguǒ . . . de huà*
跟……结婚	*gēn . . . jiéhūn*
在……时	*zài . . . shí*
跟……打交道	*gēn . . . dǎ jiāodào*
得到……认同	*dédào . . . rèntóng*
跟……相处	*gēn . . . xiāngchǔ*

1.10 理想的伴侣 Ideal Partners—我的理想的丈夫 My Ideal Husband—Level B

B

理想的丈夫

我的理想的丈夫必须毫无保留地爱我，他也必须是充满同情心的人，在他的眼中，每一个人都是重要的，他应该使人感到他对人的热爱。

他也应该有坚定的信念，如果是他所坚信的事情，他就应该永不退却，奋力争取。

他也应该很愿意与我讨论文学、哲学等等严肃的话题，或者是我喜欢的电视节目这样的轻松话题。

他应该对获取知识有强烈的渴望，因为对我来说，能够与我的终身伴侣一起来探索知识和共同成长是非常重要的。

他也应该是一个很有趣的人，因为我自己不是一个刻板严肃的人，所以他有没有幽默感是非常重要的。

我的生活目标是到全世界各地去旅行，所以我的丈夫也必须喜爱旅行，那样我们就可以一起去看世界上五彩缤纷的不同的文化和历史。

我的理想的丈夫也应当是我的最好的朋友，让我们一起去体验人生。

生词与短语 **Words and Phrases 1.10 B**

丈夫	*zhàngfu*	husband
毫无	*háowú*	without the slightest . . .
保留	*bǎoliú*	hold back
充满	*chōngmǎn*	full of . . .
同情心	*tóngqíngxīn*	sympathetic heart; kindhearted
在 . . . . . . 的眼中	*zài . . . de yǎn zhōng*	in (somebody's) eyes
使人	*shǐ rén*	make people . . .
热爱	*rè ài*	deep love or affection
坚定	*jiāndìng*	firm; steadfast
信念	*xìn-niàn*	conviction; faith
坚信	*jiānxìn*	firmly believe
永不	*yǒngbù*	never
退却	*tuìquè*	withdraw from; retreat
奋力	*fènlì*	do all one can; spare no effort
争取	*zhēngqǔ*	strive for; fight for
与	*yǔ*	with (more formal way of saying 跟 or 和)
讨论	*tǎolùn*	discuss
严肃	*yánsù*	serious
话题	*huàtí*	subject or topic of conversation
轻松	*qīngsōng*	lighthearted; relaxed

获取	*huòqǔ*	obtain
知识	*zhīshi*	knowledge
强烈	*qiángliè*	intense; strong
渴望	*kěwàng*	thirst for something
对我来说	*duì wǒ lái shuō*	as far as I'm concerned
终身	*zhōngshēn*	lifelong; all one's life
伴侣	*bànlǚ*	companion; mate; partner
探索	*tànsuǒ*	explore
共同	*gòngtóng*	together; jointly
成长	*chéngzhǎng*	grow; mature
刻板	*kèbǎn*	stiff; inflexible
幽默感	*yōumògǎn*	sense of humor
目标	*mùbiāo*	goal; aim; objective
五彩缤纷	*wǔcǎibīnfēn*	colorful
不同	*bùtóng*	not the same
体验	*tǐyàn*	personally experience
人生	*rénshēng*	(human) life

1.10 Exercise 1—Planning Your Paragraphs

Review the vocabulary and phrases you need as you plan each paragraph of your essay. Read through the models again and note key vocabulary for each paragraph in the blue spaces below.

Paragraph 1: Give a physical description of your ideal partner and the personality traits you're looking for.

Paragraph 2: Describe the interests and talents you would wish for in a partner.

Paragraph 3: Talk about what would make this person special in your eyes.

Writing about an Ideal Partner

Step 1: Reread the model texts. Mark which phrases you intend to adopt and adapt.

Step 2: Referring to the models and using your vocabulary and phrases from this exercise, draft your essay one paragraph at a time.

Terms for Family Members

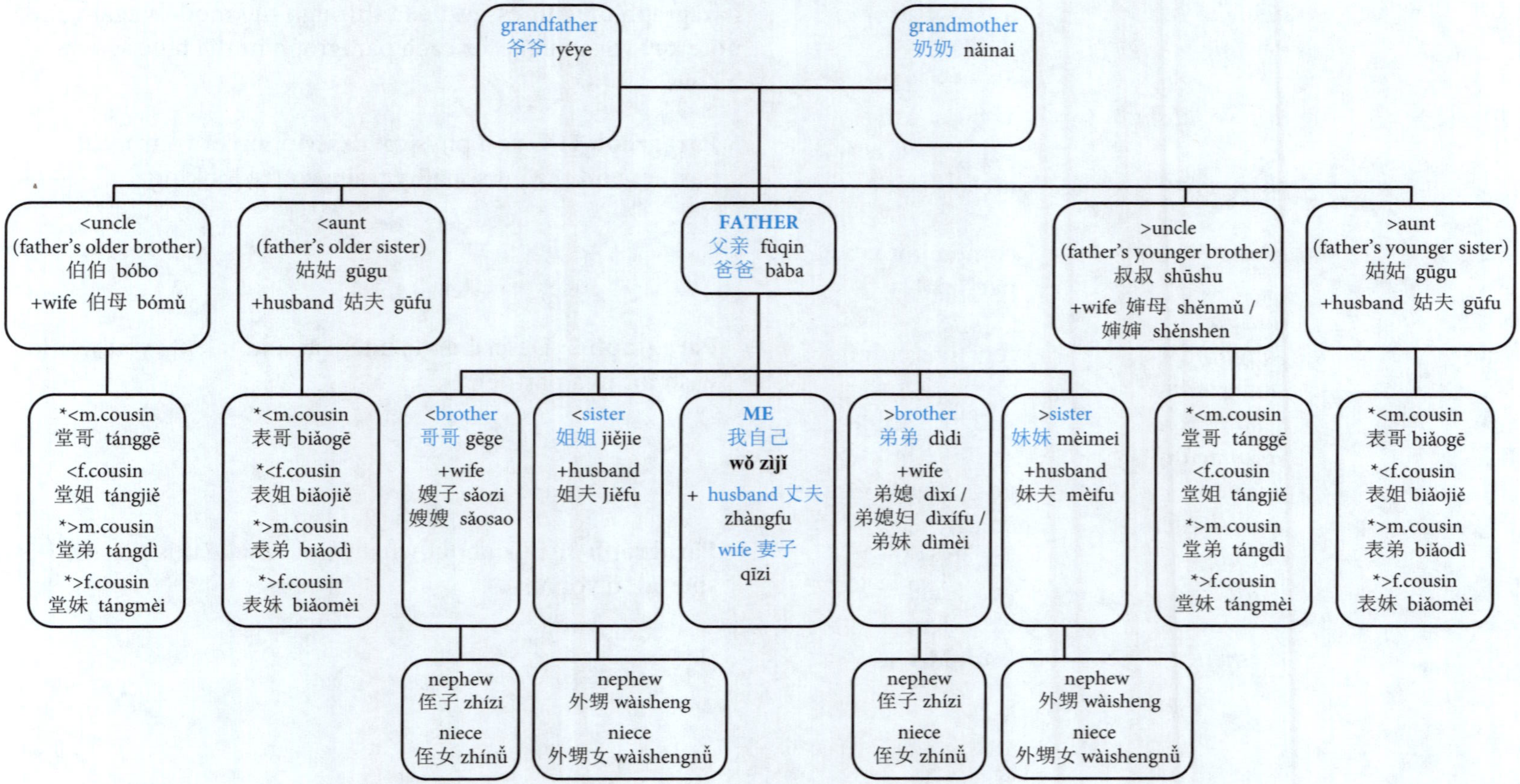

注 Notes

1. Traditionally in Chinese cultures, your father and his brothers would live in a multigenerational family compound, whereas your father's sisters would leave their family to join the husband's family compound. The unique terms used to refer to cousins from your father's brothers, in contrast to all your other possible cousins, underscores the relevance of the relatives on your father's side in relation to your mother's side and in relation to the children of your father's sisters.

Terms for Family Members

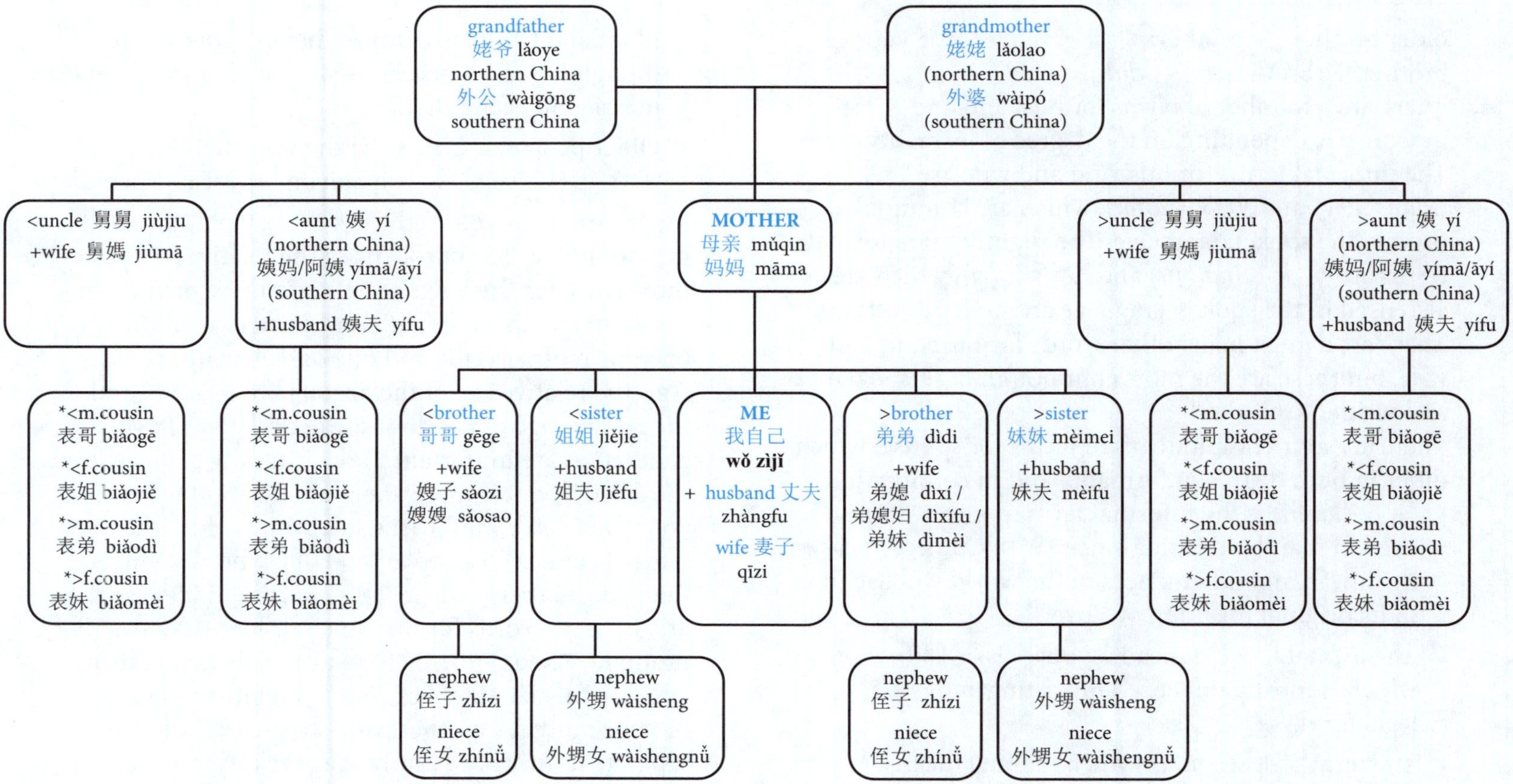

2. As indicated in the family vocabulary table above, there are sometimes different terms in use in northern and southern China.
3. Traditionally in Chinese cultures, the age of a person makes a difference in status or role in the family. That includes the relative age of the siblings in a family, which determines their status within the family. The language reflects these important cultural distinctions. For example, there are different words for your older sister [*<sister: 姐姐 *jiějie*, where the asterisk refers to yourself] and your younger sister [*>sister: 妹妹 *mèimei*], just as there are different terms for an

Terms for Family Members

older brother [*<brother: 哥哥 *gēge*] versus a younger brother [*>brother: 弟弟 *dìdi*].

4. There are a number of terms for husband and wife in Chinese, depending on the degree of formality. The informal terms for husband and wife are 先生 (*xiānsheng*) and 太太 (*tàitai*), which are commonly used in the spoken language. The slightly more formal terms are 丈夫 (*zhàngfu*) and 妻子 (*qīzi*), which are also used in the spoken language and in legal settings. There are a great many other words for husband and wife, but these are the most common in both spoken and written Chinese.
5. There are four commonly used terms for spouse, which differ in both degree of formality and in connotation.
   - 爱人 (*àirén*) is the informal term to mean "spouse" used in mainland China since 1950. Chinese speakers in Taiwan and other places in the world still use this in its original meaning of "lover."
   - The formal term to mean "spouse" is 配偶 (*pèi-ǒu*), which is mostly only used in writing and is a legal term.
   - The term 伴侣 (*bànlǚ*), which literally means "companion," comes close to the contemporary English term "significant other." Younger people in Mainland China use this to mean "spouse," even though it doesn't necessarily imply that the people are married to each other.
   - Older people in China use the informal term 老伴儿 (*lǎobàr*), "old companion," to mean "spouse."
6. The relatives on your father's side may play an importantly different role from the relatives on your mother's side. The language reflects these distinctions. For example, there are different words for an uncle on your mother's side and one on your father's side. And the relative age of the brothers in a family and the relative age of you to the other relatives in your generation are important in determining status within the family. For example, there are different words for your uncle on your father's side who is older than your father [<uncle: 伯伯 *bóbo*] and one who is younger than your father [>uncle: 叔叔 *shūshu*]. Likewise there are different words for the cousins older than you. For example, when referring to your female first cousins who are the daughters of either you father's sister or your mother's brothers or sisters, there are two separate terms based on their age relative to you [*<f.cousin: 表姐 *biǎojiě*] and younger than you [*>f.cousin: 表妹 *biǎomèi*].

第二章 Descriptions of Places and Things 描写地点和事物 2

2.1 住所 Homes—我们家的房子 My Home—Levels A and B

生词与短语 Words and Phrases 2.1 A

座	*zuò*	measure word for houses
台	*tái*	measure word for machines, including TVs and computers
聊天	*liáotiān*	chat
洗手间	*xǐshǒujiān*	washroom
洗澡间	*xǐzǎojiān*	bathroom; shower room
比较	*bǐjiào*	comparatively; relatively
靠	*kào*	just next to; alongside
车房	*chēfáng*	garage
辆	*liàng*	measure word for automobiles

2.1 Exercise 1—Reading Check

- Read the model text on this page carefully. Sketch below the floor plan for the first and second floors of the house as described in the text. Draw lines from the rooms in the text to the rooms in your floor plan. Compare your floor plan with that of a classmate.

A

我们家的房子

我们的家是一座有两层楼的房子。一楼的中间是前门，前门的右边是客厅。客厅里有两张双人沙发、一张小桌子和一台很大的电视机。我的家人在客厅里看电视或者跟客人聊天。客厅的后面是书房，里面有书桌，书桌上面是一台电脑。我的家人在书房用电脑、看书，等等。前门的左边是厨房，里面有一张饭桌和四把椅子。因为我们的房子没有饭厅，所以我们不但在厨房里做饭，也在那里吃饭。厨房的后头是个洗手间。

卧室都在楼上。二楼的右边是我的卧室。我的卧室里头有一张双人床、一张书桌和两个衣柜。我妹妹的卧室在我的卧室的右边，中间是个洗澡间。我们父母的卧室在二楼的左边。父母的卧室后头是个洗澡间。

我们的房子后面有很大的后院，有一个小花园和很多树。房子前头也有个比较小的前院。房子旁边靠厨房那一边是车房，里面有两辆车子。

生词与短语 Words and Phrases 2.1 B

壁炉	*bìlú*	fireplace
平板电视	*píngbǎn diànshì*	flat-screen TV
进入	*jìnrù*	enter
带纱窗的门廊	*dài shāchuāng de ménláng*	screened-in porch
洗碗池	*xǐwǎnchí*	kitchen sink (for washing dishes)
烤箱	*kǎoxiāng*	oven
冰箱	*bīngxiāng*	refrigerator
微波炉	*wēibōlú*	microwave
碗橱	*wǎnchú*	cupboard
全家人	*quán jiā rén*	the entire family
待	*dāi*	stay
扇	*shàn*	measure word for doors (a leaf of a door)
对面	*duìmiàn*	across from; facing
木制	*mùzhì*	wooden
平台	*píngtái*	patio; deck
浴室	*yùshì*	bathroom (synonymous with洗澡间; see Note 2)
淋浴	*línyù*	shower
马桶	*mǎtǒng*	toilet; commode
洗手池	*xǐshǒuchí*	bathroom sink; wash basin
台灯	*táidēng*	table lamp
沙发椅	*shāfāyǐ*	upholstered armchair
梳妆台	*shūzhuāngtái*	dressing table; vanity
壁橱	*bìchú*	closet

B

我家的房子

我们家的房子是一座白色的房子，离我们的大学很近。

从前门一进来，你就会看到客厅，客厅里靠窗户有两张双人沙发、两把椅子、一张咖啡桌。壁炉上面有一个很大的平板电视，靠墙有一个很大的书架。从客厅前面可以进入到带纱窗的门廊里去。

客厅的旁边是饭厅，里面有一张大饭桌和六把椅子。从饭厅的窗户向外看，就可以看到后院子。

饭厅的旁边是厨房，里面有洗碗池、烤箱、冰箱、微波炉。墙上有很多碗橱。因为我的家人都喜欢做饭，所以我们全家人都很喜欢待在厨房里。这里也有一扇门可以进到车房里去。

厨房的对面是一个卧室，里面有两张单人床和两张书桌。这是我的两个弟弟的房间，从这里可以走到后院里的木制平台上去。

弟弟的卧室旁边是一个浴室，里面有淋浴、马桶和洗手池。

我的卧室在浴室的后边，里面有一张双人床，床前有一张小桌子和台灯，靠窗有一张书桌和一把椅子。

楼下是我父母的卧室，这也是我们家里最大的一间卧室，里面有一张非常大的床、两把沙发椅、一张梳妆台，还有一个大壁橱。

B

我父母的卧室的左边是一个大浴室，里边不但有淋浴，还有一个浴缸，也有洗手池和马桶。

我们的房子也有一个地下室，里边有洗衣机和烘干机，很多壁橱，一个暖气炉。

房子的最高处有一个很小的阁楼，里边存放着我们小的时候画的画、旧的玩具等等，我妈妈都当做宝贝一样永久保留着。

生词与短语 Words and Phrases 2.1 B

浴缸	*yùgāng*	bathtub
地下室	*dìxiàshì*	basement
烘干机	*hōng-gānjī*	clothes dryer
暖气炉	*nuǎnqìlú*	furnace
阁楼	*gélóu*	attic
存放	*cúnfàng*	to store; keep
宝贝	*bǎobèi*	treasure
永久	*yǒngjiǔ*	forever
保留	*bǎoliú*	keep; retain (in a different context, 保留 can be used to mean "hold back")

注 Notes

1. Whenever measure words are involved, it is incorrect to write Arabic numbers before the noun. For example, 两层楼 is correct, although in informal contexts, such as e-mail or on social media, you may see 2层楼.
2. Just as in English, there are many words for *bathroom* in Chinese. In this book, we have deliberately used a variety of those terms. There is a difference between them, however. The terms 浴室 (*yùshì*) and 洗澡间 (*xǐzǎojiān*) can only be used in referring to bathrooms in private homes or hotel rooms and not in public places, since they refer to places where you can bathe. 洗手间 (*xǐshǒujiān*), 卫生间 (*wèishēngjiān*), and 厕所 (*cèsuǒ*) are similar to the words *washroom*, *lavatory*, and *toilet*, respectively, and generally refer to spaces in public places. However, if a home has a half bath, with a sink and toilet but no bathtub or shower, it is called a 洗手间. Rarely is 厕所 used these days to refer to a toilet in a private apartment in the city, as those spaces tend to include a bathing area as well.

注 Notes

3. 因为……所以……　*yīnwéi . . . suóyǐ*　because . . . , (so) . . .
In Chinese, unlike in English, when a sentence begins with the word *because* (*yīnwéi*), the second clause generally begins with the word *so* or *therefore* (*suóyǐ*) in cases of cause and effect. This is but one example of the kind of parallel construction common in the Chinese language.

例句 Example Sentences

因为今天下大雨了，所以我们不能去散步。
Yīnwei jīntiān xià dà yǔ le, suǒyǐ wǒmen bùnéng qù sànbù.
Because it's raining hard today, we can't go for a walk.

因为明天有考试，所以我今天晚上得复习。
Yīnwei míngtiān yǒu kǎoshì, suǒyǐ wǒ jīntiān wǎnshàng děi fùxí.
Because there's a test tomorrow, so this evening I have to review.

4. 当做……一样　*dàngzuò. . . yíyàng*　to treat/regard as . . .

例句 Example Sentences

我已经18岁了，可是母亲还是把我当做小孩子一样！
Wǒ yǐjīng shíbāsuìle, kěshì mǔqīn háishì bǎ wǒ dàngzuò xiǎo háizi yíyàng!
I'm already eighteen years old, but (my) mother still treats me like a little kid!

弟弟把妈妈的劝告当做废话一样。
Dìdi bǎ māma de quàngào dàngzuò fèihuà yíyàng.
My little brother regards my mother's advice as nonsense.

2.1 Exercise 2—Vocab Grab

Review the model text(s) in this section and grab the vocabulary items related to rooms and furniture that you might use in your own text about your home.

2.1 Exercise 3—Writing about Your Own Home—Drafting

Brainstorm Your Essay
Sketch the exterior of your house and the floor plan of your home.

Writing about Your Own Home
Step 1: Compose your essay following the steps on this page.
Step 2: Have someone proofread your essay. Ask him or her to check your description of the house against the floor plan that you drafted.
Step 3: Edit and polish your essay before handing it in for feedback, assessment, or adding to your writing portfolio.

Paragraph 1: Exterior of the House
Describe the outside appearance of the house, including the number of floors, the relative size, and color(s) on the outside. Describe the front and back yards of the house, the location of the garage, and so on.

Paragraph 2: Interior of the House
Describe the layout of the rooms in the house, starting with what lies to the right and left of the front door on the first floor. Give the location of each room in relation to the rooms next to it, either in front or behind, to the right or the left. Include a description of the furniture in each room.

If the house has more than one floor, describe the layout of rooms on the second floor, including the important pieces of furniture. For the bedrooms, mention which room belongs to which member of the family.

2.2 住所 Homes—我的宿舍的房间 My Dorm Room—Level A

A

我的宿舍的房间

我的宿舍的房间很普通，但是我和我的同屋合作得很好。为了能有更多的空间，我和我的同屋把我们的两张床架在书桌和衣橱的上面的墙上，然后我们把房间分成两个活动范围：房间的右边是他的活动范围，房间的左边是我的，我们可以按照个人的爱好来装饰自己的活动范围。

我在我自己的活动范围有一个小冰箱，书架上有我所有的课本。我的同屋在他的活动范围里有一个很舒适的小沙发，他喜欢坐在沙发上念书。

房间里的地毯是褐色的，墙是白色的，天花板也是白色的。我们在墙上挂了很多不同国家的国旗，因为我们都喜欢旅行，每去过一个国家，我们就把那个国家的国旗挂在墙上，红红绿绿的，把房间装点得很喜庆。房间里还有一个电扇，墙上有两个壁橱。窗子正对着网球场。

我们的宿舍房间很简单，但是很有家的感觉。

生词与短语 **Words and Phrases 2.2 A**

普通	*pǔtōng*	ordinary; common; average
同屋	*tóngwū*	roommate
合作	*hézuò*	cooperate; work together
为了	*wèile*	in order to; for the sake of
空间	*kōngjiān*	space
架	*jià*	prop up on; support
衣橱	*yīchú*	wardrobe (free-standing closet)
然后	*ránhòu*	and then; after that
分成	*fēnchéng*	divide into
活动	*huódòng*	activity
范围	*fànwéi*	scope; prescribed area
按照	*ànzhào*	according to
个人	*gèrén*	individual (person)
爱好	*àihào*	interests; hobbies
装饰	*zhuāngshì*	decorate
所有的	*suǒyǒude*	all
舒适	*shūshì*	comfortable; cozy
地毯	*dìtǎn*	carpet
褐色	*hèsè*	brown
天花板	*tiānhuābǎn*	ceiling
挂	*guà*	hang; put up
不同	*bùtóng*	not the same
国旗	*guóqí*	national flag
红红绿绿的	*hónghóng lǜlǜde*	colorful
装点	*zhuāngdiǎn*	decorate; dress up
喜庆	*xǐqìng*	joyous
电扇	*diànshàn*	electric fan
壁橱	*bìchú*	(built-in) closet

→

生词与短语 **Words and Phrases 2.2 A**

网球场	*wǎngqiúchǎng*	tennis court(s)
简单	*jiǎndān*	simple
感觉	*gǎnjué*	feeling

2.2 住所 Homes—我的宿舍的房间 My Dorm Room—Level B

B

宿舍的房间

我和我的同屋分用同一个宿舍房间。我们也分用一张双层床，我的同屋睡在下铺，因为她喜欢早起。她有蓝色的被子和非常大的枕头。我睡上铺，我有白色的被子和一床米色的毯子。

门的两边的墙上挂了好几张画，我们也把圣诞节的彩灯挂在四面的墙上，虽然这有点可笑，但是这样晚上我们躺在床上就可以看到美丽的彩色灯光，别的来我们的房间玩的同学都说很好看。

在彩灯的下面有两张书桌。书桌上堆满了课本**啊**、各种各样的笔**啊**、还有似乎永远也做不完的作业。壁橱在门的左边的那面墙上，里边放满了衣服和鞋子。我的衣服是按照颜色来分放的。我的同屋的衣服却是按照衣服的种类来分放的。

(Continues on the next page.)

生词与短语 **Words and Phrases 2.2 B**

分用	*fēnyòng*	share
双层床	*shuāngcéngchuáng*	bunk bed
下铺	*xiàpù*	lower berth
早起	*zǎoqǐ*	to get up early
枕头	*zhěntou*	pillow
床	*chuáng*	measure word for blankets and quilts
米色	*mǐsè*	cream-colored
毯子	*tǎnzi*	blanket
圣诞节	*Shèngdànjié*	Christmas
彩灯	*cǎidēng*	colored lights
四面	*sìmiàn*	all four sides (of a wall)
可笑	*kěxiào*	laughable; ridiculous
彩色	*cǎisè*	multicolored
灯光	*dēng-guāng*	lamplight
堆满	*duīmǎn*	piled up
各种各样的	*gèzhǒng gèyàngde*	every kind of
似乎	*sìhū*	seems like; as if
壁橱	*bìchú*	closet
按照	*ànzhào*	according to
分放	*fēn fàng*	placed down in separate places
却	*què*	however; actually (contrary to expectation)
种类	*zhǒnglèi*	types; kinds; varieties

(宿舍的房间 *continued*)

壁橱的旁边的架子上有很多我计划在这个学期要读的小说，我的同屋的书则大部分是科学幻想小说。

我们的浴室有点乱，美容和美发用品堆满了洗手池的台子上，清洁用品挤满了洗手池的下边。虽然我和我的同屋每周轮流清洁浴室，但是我们的浴室还是很乱。

生词与短语 Words and Phrases 2.2 B (*continued*)

架子	*jiàzi*	shelf
则	*zé*	on the other hand
科学幻想小说	*kēxué huànxiǎng xiǎoshuō*	science-fiction novels
乱	*luàn*	disorderly
美容和美发用品	*měiróng hé měifà yòngpǐn*	cosmetic and hair products; beauty products
洗手池	*xǐshǒuchí*	(bathroom) sink
台子	*táizi*	counter (of the sink)
清洁用品	*qīngjié yòngpǐn*	cleaning products
挤满	*jǐmǎn*	crammed; packed full
轮流	*lúnliú*	take turns

2.2 Exercise 1—Reading Check

Check your comprehension of the model text(s) on the previous two pages by answering the questions below.

Level A

- How do the writer and the writer's roommate get along?
- Where does the writer's roommate like to study?

Level B

- Which bunk does the writer sleep in?
- What is hanging on the walls of the dorm room?

注 Notes

1. The Taiwanese word for roommate, 室友 *shìyǒu*, is increasingly popular in China.

注 Notes

2. Use this phrase to enumerate items:
   ......啊......啊 ... *a* ... *a* things like ... and ... (etc.)

   例句 Example Sentences

   书桌上有书**啊**、笔记本**啊**、笔**啊**什么的。
   Shūzhuōshàng yǒu shū a, bǐjìběn a, bǐ a shénmede.
   On the desk there are things like books, notebooks, pens, and so on.

   床上有枕头**啊**、被子**啊**、毯子等等很多东西。
   Chuángshàng yǒu zhěntou a, bèizi a, tǎnzi děngděng hěnduō dōngxi.
   On the bed there are a lot of things, like a pillow, a comforter, a blanket, etc.

   Use the phrase ......啊......啊 to write a sentence in which you enumerate the things in your backpack or closet.

2.3 住所 Homes—我的公寓 My Apartment—Level B

生词与短语 Words and Phrases 2.3 B

公寓	*gōngyù*	apartment
大三	*dàsān*	third-year university student
校外	*xiàowài*	outside of school; off-campus
租	*zū*	rent (verb)
包括	*bāokuò*	include
互联网	*hùliánwǎng*	the internet
水电费	*shuǐdiànfèi*	the utilities
分担	*fēndān*	share responsibility for
费用	*fèiyòng*	cost; expense
相当	*xiāngdāng*	quite; fairly
养	*yǎng*	raise
猫	*māo*	cat(s)
遗憾	*yíhàn*	regret
许	*xǔ*	allow; permit
宠物	*chǒngwù*	household pet
L形状的	*L xíngzhuàngde*	L-shaped
不成问题	*bùchéng wèntí*	not a problem
手机	*shǒujī*	cell phone
保持	*bǎochí*	keep; maintain
联系	*liánxì*	contact
戴	*dài*	put on; wear
耳机	*ěrjī*	earphone
沙发椅	*shāfāyǐ*	upholstered armchair
面对着	*miànduìzhe*	facing; across from
平板电视	*píngbǎn diànshì*	flat-screen TV
周末	*zhōumò*	weekend
玩儿电脑游戏	*wánr diànnǎo yóuxì*	play computer games
不愁	*bùchóu*	not worry about

B

我们的公寓

我是一个大三的学生，所以我可以住在校外的公寓里。我租的公寓离我们的大学很近，走路只需要十分钟，如果开车只需要三分钟。

每个月房租是一千五百块，这包括互联网Wi-Fi和水电费。因为我和我的另外两个朋友分担这个费用， 所以我们都觉得房租相当便宜。虽然我喜欢养猫，遗憾的是这里不许养宠物。

我们的公寓有三个卧室、一个厨房、一个客厅和一个浴室。你一进到公寓就是我们的客厅，客厅里有一张L形状的长沙发，坐四、五个人不成问题。平常我喜欢坐在沙发上<u>一边</u>做我的作业，<u>一边</u>用我的手机跟我的朋友保持联系。当然我也会戴着耳机听我的iPod。客厅里还有三把沙发椅，这三把沙发椅和L形状的长沙发都面对着一台很大的平板电视，所以周末的时候我们的朋友们来我们这里一起玩儿电脑游戏、看DVD的时候，也不愁没有地方坐。

(Continues on the next page.)

B

(我们的公寓 *continued*)

客厅的右边是厨房。厨房尽头是一张四方桌和四把椅子，我们平常就在那里吃饭。厨房的左边有一个很大的冰箱，冰箱的旁边是煤气炉，墙上有很多碗橱，厨房的右边有烤箱和洗碗机。虽然厨房里的设备很齐全， 但是我们三个男生都不太喜欢做饭， 所以我们早上吃点麦片、烤面包什么的；中午用生菜、西红柿、火腿和面包做个三明治填饱肚子，晚上我们就订比萨饼等等外卖。

客厅的左边是浴室，里面有淋浴啊、马桶啊、洗手池啊什么的。

公寓的后半部分就是我们的三间卧室。我的卧室里有一张大床、一张单人沙发和一盏落地灯。

我觉得住在这里很舒适，我和我的朋友的关系很和谐，我们都对我们的公寓很满意。

生词与短语 Words and Phrases 2.3 B (*continued*)

尽头	*jìntóu*	the back of; end
四方桌	*sìfāng zhuō*	square table
煤气炉	*méiqìlú*	gas stove
墙	*qiáng*	wall
碗橱	*wǎnchú*	cupboard
洗碗机	*xǐwǎnjī*	dishwasher
设备	*shèbèi*	facilities
齐全	*qíquán*	complete
麦片	*màipiàn*	cereal
烤面包	*kǎomiànbāo*	toast
什么的	*shénme de*	and so on
生菜	*shēngcài*	lettuce
西红柿	*xīhóngshì*	tomato
火腿	*huǒtuǐ*	ham
三明治	*sānmíngzhì*	sandwich
填饱肚子	*tiánbǎo dùzi*	fill the stomach
订	*dìng*	order (merchandise, food, etc.)
比萨饼	*bǐsàbǐng*	pizza
等等	*děng děng*	etc.
外卖	*wàimài*	takeout (food)
淋浴	*línyù*	shower
马桶	*mǎtǒng*	toilet; commode
洗手池	*xǐshǒuchí*	(bathroom) sink
后半部分	*hòubàn bùfen*	the back half
单人沙发	*dānrén shāfā*	large deep upholstered armchair
盏	*zhǎn*	measure word for lamps
落地灯	*luòdìdēng*	floor lamp
舒适	*shūshì*	comfortable; cozy
和谐	*héxié*	harmonious

2.3 Exercise 1—Reading Check

Read the statements below about the text "My Apartment." Place a checkmark by the statements that are correct. Circle what is incorrect in the inaccurate statements.

________ The apartment rent includes utilities.

________ The roommates have a cat.

________ The writer avoids doing homework in the living room.

________ The roommates love to cook big meals in their kitchen.

________ The roommates are satisfied with their apartment.

2.3 Exercise 2—Which Word Doesn't Belong?

Circle the words that don't belong in each of the categories.

Foods

比萨饼	*bǐsàbǐng*
碗橱	*wǎnchú*
烤面包	*kǎomiànbāo*
西红柿	*xīhóngshì*

Furniture

落地灯	*luòdìdēng*
沙发椅	*shāfāyǐ*
四方桌	*sìfāng zhuō*
手机	*shǒujī*

Appliances

墙	*qiáng*
洗碗机	*xǐwǎnjī*
煤气炉	*méiqìlú*
舒适	*shūshì*

注 Notes

1. A parallel construction for two simultaneous actions (doing one thing while doing another):
一边……一边…… *yìbiān ... yìbiān ...*

例句 Example Sentences

我一边吃饭，一边看电视。
Wǒ yìbiān chīfàn, yìbiān kàn diànshì.
I eat while watching TV.

我一边做作业，一边听音乐。
Wǒ yìbiān zuò zuòyè, yìbiān tīng yīnyuè.
I do my homework while listening to music.

2. Expressing satisfaction or dissatisfaction:
对……满意/不满意 *duì ... mǎnyì* be satisfied or dissatisfied with ...

例句 Example Sentences

我对我的宿舍的设备很满意。
Wǒ duì wǒde sùshè de shèbèi hěn mǎnyì.
I'm satisfied with the facilities in my dorm.

很多美国人对自己的政府的政策不满意。
Hěnduō Měiguó rén duì zìjǐde zhèngfǔ de zhèngcè bùmǎnyì.
Many Americans are dissatisfied with their own government's policies.

2.3 Exercise 3—How Satisfied Are You with Life at Your University or College?

Circle your responses, then share your responses (in Chinese) with others in your class.

			Very satisfied			Very dissatisfied	
宿舍的房间	*sùshè de fángjiān*	dorm room	5	4	3	2	1
同屋	*tóngwū*	roommate	5	4	3	2	1
床	*chuáng*	bed	5	4	3	2	1
浴室	*yùshì*	bathroom	5	4	3	2	1
学习的地方	*xuéxí de dìfang*	places to study	5	4	3	2	1
自助餐厅的食物	*zìzhù cāntīng de shíwù*	cafeteria food	5	4	3	2	1

2.3 Exercise 4—Writing about Your Own Dorm Room or Apartment—Text Building

Plan your paragraphs	Grab key vocab and phrases from the models in this section
Paragraph 1: People • your roommate(s) • your activities in the room or apartment	
Paragraph 2: Rooms • size of room(s) • color of walls • decoration	
Paragraph 3: Furniture • pieces of furniture in the room(s) • where the pieces of furniture are located in relation to one another	
Paragraph 4: Opinions • aspects of your living situation that you are satisfied or not satisfied with	

Writing about Your Own Home

Step 1: Compose your essay using the words and phrases in the text builder on this page.

Step 2: Have someone proofread your essay. If you can, invite them to your dorm room or apartment to check the accuracy of your description!

Step 3: Edit and polish your essay before handing it in for feedback, assessment, or adding to your writing portfolio.

2.4 我居住的地方 Where I Live—我们的校园 My Campus—Levels A and B

生词与短语 Words and Phrases 2.4 A

校园	*xiàoyuán*	campus
穿过	*chuānguò*	pass through
所	*suǒ*	measure word for buildings, etc.
头一 座楼	*tóu yízuò lóu*	the first of the buildings
行政楼	*xíngzhènglóu*	administration building
学生活动中心	*xuéshēng huódòng zhōngxīn*	student activities center; student union
咖啡厅	*kāfēitīng*	coffee shop
聊天	*liáotiān*	chat
体育馆	*tǐyùguǎn*	gymnasium
排球场	*páiqiúchǎng*	volleyball court
举重练习场	*jǔzhòng liànxí chǎng*	weight-lifting exercise place (weight room)
教学楼	*jiàoxuélóu*	classroom building

A

我们的校园

我觉得我们大学的校园很美。校园里有很多树和花儿，也有一条小河穿过校园的中间。因为这所大学一共有四千个学生，所以校园也比较大。一进到校园，头一座楼就是行政楼。那座楼的后头就是学生活动中心，里面有咖啡厅和一个大厅，大厅里面有沙发、书桌，等等，学生们可以在那儿念书、跟朋友聊天、休息。学生活动中心的右边是图书馆。图书馆有六层楼，电脑中心在一楼。学生活动中心的左边有学生餐厅和大学书店。活动中心后面有一个很大的体育馆，里面有游泳池、篮球场、排球场和举重练习场。图书馆的前头和后头是教学楼。科学系、数学系和地理系的教室和教授的办公室都在图书馆的后头。英文系、历史系、外语系和艺术系的教室和教授的办公室都在图书馆前头。学生宿舍在餐厅的前头和后头。我很喜欢我们大学的校园。

2.4 Exercise 1—Reading Check

Place a checkmark next to the campus locations mentioned in the text on this page:

_____ administration building

_____ classrooms

_____ dormitory

_____ student union

_____ gymnasium

_____ coffee shop

2.4 Exercise 2—Where Do You Spend Time on Campus?

How often do you visit the following campus locations? Circle 4 for "daily," 3 for "weekly," 2 for "monthly," and 1 for "never."

行政楼	*xíngzhènglóu*	4	3	2	1
学生活动中心	*xuéshēng huódòng zhōngxīn*	4	3	2	1
咖啡厅	*kāfēitīng*	4	3	2	1
教学楼	*jiàoxuélóu*	4	3	2	1
体育馆	*tǐyùguǎn*	4	3	2	1
宿舍	*sùshè*	4	3	2	1
图书馆	*túshūguǎn*	4	3	2	1

注 Notes for page 48

1. Even just a few decades ago, the tendency was to write all numbers in Chinese characters. For example, 50 percent was commonly written as 百分之五十. However, using Chinese characters for numbers has recently fallen out of favor. Now Arabic numerals and symbols are most often used when numbers are involved. It isn't wrong to use Chinese characters to write numbers. What is incorrect, though, is to mix Arabic numbers with Chinese characters for numbers. For example, 百分之50 is definitely wrong.
2. American-style football is called 橄榄球 (literally "olive ball," based on the shape of the ball) in mainland China, but 美式足球 is often used by the Chinese in the United States to differentiate 足球 ("world football" or "soccer") from American football. In later texts in this book we deliberately use the term 美式足球 to show the term more commonly used in the United States.

B

美丽的校园

我们的大学的校园位于美国中西部的一个小城里，校园非常大，几乎百分之五十的小城的市中心都属于我们的校园。

图书馆是一座八层高的白色大楼，从市中心的任何一个角度都能看到。科学楼在校园的最西边，形状很奇特，好像是一个数学无穷符号∞。语言教学楼是一座圆形的大楼，位于校园的最东边，英语系和中文系都在这栋大楼里。

校园的中间是一个小湖，学生下了课以后就可以到湖上划船、做帆板运动、游泳。小湖前面是一片大草坪，春夏秋三个季节都有不同的鲜花开放。学生们很喜欢坐在草坪上和朋友聊天、做阳光浴、玩飞碟，等等。

历史系大楼的旁边是一个有名的博物馆，每年都有成千上万的人从全国各地来参观。政治学系和教育系的大楼的后边是体育场，我们的大学的橄榄球队和其他大学的比赛就在这里举行。

要是你问我校园里最有意思的地方是什么，我就会告诉你学生们最喜欢的地方之一就是学生活动中心大楼，里面有乒乓球台、台球台、桌式足球等等。

生词与短语 **Words and Phrases 2.4 B**

位于	*wèiyú*	be located in; be situated in
中西部	*zhōngxībù*	Midwest
百分之五十	*bǎifēn zhī wǔshí*	50 percent
属于	*shǔyú*	belong to; be part of
座	*zuò*	measure word for large structures
任何	*rènhé*	any
角度	*jiǎodù*	angle; point of view
形状	*xíngzhuàng*	form; shape
奇特	*qítè*	unique
无穷符号	*wúqióng fúhào*	symbol for infinity
圆形	*yuánxíng*	circular; round
栋	*dòng*	measure for buildings
划船	*huáchuán*	row a boat
帆板	*fānbǎn*	windsurfing
片	*piàn*	measure word for lawn
草坪	*cǎopíng*	lawn
不同	*bùtóng*	not the same
鲜花	*xiānhuā*	fresh flowers
开放	*kāifàng*	bloom; open
阳光浴	*yáng-guāngyù*	sunbathing
飞碟	*fēidié*	Frisbee
成千上万	*chéngqiān shàngwàn*	by the thousands
参观	*cānguān*	visit (a place such as a museum or school)
政治学	*zhèngzhìxué*	political science
橄榄球队	*gǎnlǎnqíu duì*	football team
举行	*jǔxíng*	hold (an event)
……之一	*zhī yī*	one of the . . .
乒乓球台	*pīngpāngqiú tái*	ping-pong table
台球台	*táiqiú tái*	billiard table
桌式足球	*zhuōshì zúqiú*	foosball

B

由于我们的校园在市中心，所以校园附近有很多家有异国风情的小餐馆，价格不但相当便宜，而且很可口。附近还有三家电影院，经常上演外国电影。

我们大学的同学们都为我们的美丽校园感到骄傲。

生词与短语 Words and Phrases 2.4 B

由于	*yóuyú*	due to the fact that
异国风情	*yìguó fēngqíng*	foreign atmosphere
相当	*xiāngdāng*	quite; fairly
可口	*kěkǒu*	tasty
上演	*shàngyǎn*	perform; to show
为 someone/something 感到骄傲	*wèi* [somebody/something] *gǎndào jiāoào*	feel proud of someone or something

2.4 Exercise 3—Writing about Your Own Campus—Drafting

Grab vocab from the model texts that you can use in a description of your own and write it in the appropriate boxes.

1. **Location:** Give the location (city and state) and relative size of your campus. Describe notable scenes and landscape features on the campus, such as a lake, river, woods, central green space, and so on.

2. **Buildings:** Describe the buildings at your school, starting with a central point like an administration building or lake or river. Mention the number of dorms, cafeterias, the library, and so on. Give their location relative to the central point you chose.

3. **Academics:** Give the relative location of various departments and classroom buildings, including the building that houses the Asian languages program. Describe any distinctive features of the classroom buildings on campus.

4. **Recreation:** Describe the recreational facilities on campus, including a student union or student activities center, the sports center (e.g., gym, swimming pool), and the number and type of athletic fields.

Writing about Your Campus

Compose an essay in which you address each of the topics above. End with a statement summarizing your feelings about the campus. Have someone familiar with your campus proofread it before handing it in for feedback, assessment, or adding to your writing portfolio.

2.5 我居住的地方 Where I Live—天气 Weather—Levels A and B

生词与短语 Words and Phrases 2.5 A

暖和	*nuǎnhe* (northern pronunciation: *nuǎnhuo*)	warm
舒服	*shūfu*	comfortable; to feel good
几乎	*jīhū*	almost; nearly
大晴天	*dà qíngtiān*	really nice day; very sunny day
阴天	*yīntiān*	cloudy or overcast day
特别是	*tèbiéshì*	especially
初	*. . . chū*	the beginning of . . .
刮风	*guā fēng*	to be windy
让人觉得	*ràng rén juéde*	make people feel . . .
从……一直到	*cóng . . . yìzhí dào . . .*	from . . . right up until . . .
底	*dǐ*	the end of . . .
气温	*qìwēn*	air temperature
度	*dù*	degrees
以上	*yǐshàng*	more than . . . ; above . . .

注 Notes

The temperature 20 degrees Celsius is written as 摄氏二十度 (*shèshì èrshídù*). More recently it is also written as 20°C, but it would still be read as *shèshì èrshídù*. To be scientifically correct, it should be written and said as 二十摄氏度. However, as is often the case, when many people begin writing something incorrectly, it eventually becomes the accepted way. It is still acceptable to use Chinese characters for all the numbers and symbols when expressing temperature. Keep in mind that in China, as in almost every other country in the world, Celsius is always used when stating the temperature, not Fahrenheit.

A

这里的天气

这个星期我们这里的天气真好。春天来了，所以天气暖和了。上个星期有一点冷，可是这个星期比上个星期暖和多了。而且上个星期有四天都下雨了，虽然有很多花儿开了，但是在雨里散步还是不太舒服。这个星期几乎每天都是大晴天，就是昨天是阴天。

去年五月的天气没有今年的天气那么好。特别是去年五月初的时候很冷，常常刮风，让人觉得好像春天不会来了。这里的冬天很长，从十一月一直到三月底或者四月初都经常下雪，所以春天来到的时候大家都很高兴。气温一到了20度以上就会有很多人开始穿T-恤衫和短裤。

B

四季的天气

我住在美国的中西部的一个小城市。这里的冬天非常冷，几乎每个星期都会下雪，再加上刮西北风，温度常常会降低到零下20度，出门必须戴上厚厚的棉帽子和围巾，要穿上厚厚的长靴，因为地上的雪很深，有几十英寸厚。

即使不下雪，这里冬天的时候天也常常是阴天，灰蒙蒙的天空，让人的心情也很受影响。

春天在这里非常短，如果你稍微不注意就会错过了，气温往往还是很低，而且还会有很冷的风，但是到南方去过冬的鸟儿们飞回来了。

夏天的时候这里又湿又热，往往会达到90多度，几乎每周都会下雨。但是晴天的时候，万里蓝天上飘浮着几缕白云，那是我最喜欢的日子。

秋天的时候气温下降得很快，空气也变得干燥了。树叶变成红黄色，在阳光下分外美丽。

生词与短语 Words and Phrases 2.5 B

再加上	*zài jiāshàng*	on top of all that; added to all that
刮西北风	*guā xīběi fēng*	a northwest wind blows
温度	*wēndù*	temperature
降低	*jiàngdī*	drop; lower
零下	*língxià*	below zero
戴上	*dài shang*	put on; wear (a hat, etc.)
厚	*hòu*	thick; heavy (clothing)
棉帽子	*mián màozi*	cotton-lined hat or cap
围巾	*wéijīn*	muffler; wool scarf
长靴	*chángxuē*	long boots
即使	*jíshǐ*	even if
阴天	*yīntiān*	cloudy
灰蒙蒙	*huī méngméng*	overcast
天空	*tiānkōng*	the sky
心情	*xīnqíng*	mood; frame of mind
受影响	*shòu yǐngxiǎng*	to be affected; to be influenced
稍微	*shāowēi*	a little bit; slightly
注意	*zhùyì*	pay attention; notice
错过	*cuòguò*	miss; let slip by
气温	*qìwēn*	air temperature
往往	*wǎngwǎng*	often; frequently
过冬	*guò dōng*	pass the winter
鸟儿	*niǎoer*	birds
湿	*shī*	wet; humid
达到	*dádào*	reach; attain
飘浮	*piāofú*	float
缕	*lǚ*	wisps; strands (measure word for thin, wispy clouds)
下降	*xiàjiàng*	drop; go down
空气	*kōngqì*	air
变得	*biànde*	become

生词与短语 Words and Phrases 2.5 B

干燥	*gānzào*	dry; arid
树叶	*shùyè*	(tree) leaves
变成	*biànchéng*	change into; become
阳光	*yáng-guāng*	sunlight; sunshine
分外	*fènwài*	particularly; especially

注 Notes

1. 比……多了 *A bǐ B adj. duōle* A is much more adj. than B (Always use 多了 or 多得多 in comparisons to mean "much more . . . than" rather than 很多.)	例句 **Example Sentences** Kobe Bryant 比我高多了。 *Kobe Bryant bǐ wǒ gāo duōle.* Kobe Bryant is much taller than I am. 今天比昨天热多了。 *Jīntiān bǐ zuótiān rè duōle.* Today is much hotter than yesterday.
2. 虽然……但是 *suírán . . . dànshì although . . . (but)* When the first clause in a sentence begins with 虽然 (although), the second clause generally begins with 但是 (however; but) or 可是. This is one more example of parallel construction in Chinese sentences. It may seem unnecessary in English to say "Although many flowers are blooming, *but* it's still unpleasant to take a walk in the rain," but it is correct to add the word "but" in Chinese.	例句 **Example Sentences** **虽然**小王看起来瘦瘦的，**但是**其实他身体很好。 *Suírán Xiǎo Wáng kànqǐlái shòushòude, dànshì qíshí tā shēntǐ hěn hǎo.* Although Little Wang looks really skinny, (but) he's actually in very good health. 我们的球队**虽然**尽了最大的努力，**但是**我们最后还是输了。 *Wǒmende qiúduì suírán jìnle zuìdàde nǔlì, dànshì wǒmen zuìhòu háishì shūle.* Although our (ball game) team gave it all we had, in the end we still lost.
3. 没有……那么…… *A méiyǒu B name . . . adj.* A is not adj. as B	例句 **Example Sentences** 北京的冬天**没有**芝加哥的冬天**那么**冷。 *Běijīngde dōngtiān méiyǒu Zhījiāgēde dōngtiān nàme lěng.* Beijing winters aren't as cold as Chicago winters. 这个房子**没有**那个房子**那么**贵。 *Zhèige fángzi méiyǒu nàge fángzi nàme guì.* This house isn't as expensive as that house.

2.5 Exercise 1—Comparing the Weather

Write two sentences comparing the weather in two cities. Use the structures introduced on the previous page and the weather adjectives below.

冷	*lěng*	cold
多雪	*duōxuě*	snowy
暖和	*nuǎnhe; nuǎnhuo*	warm
晴朗	*qínglǎng*	sunny
刮风	*guā fēng*	to be windy
阴天	*yīntiān*	cloudy
干燥	*gānzào*	dry; arid
湿	*shī*	wet; humid

1.

2.

注 Notes

Generally speaking, the minus sign (–) in English, which indicates temperature below zero, or the plus sign (+) to indicate temperatures above zero, normally are not used to describe temperatures in Chinese. If the temperature is 20 degrees below zero Celsius (4 degrees below zero Fahrenheit), then it is written as 零下20度, which literally means "zero below 20 degrees." If the temperature is 20 degrees above zero, it is written 20度. Only if you want to emphasize *above* zero do you write 零上20度 ("zero above 20 degrees"). Otherwise it is not necessary to write 零上.

Writing about the Weather in your Hometown

Step 1: Review the model texts and circle the weather vocabulary that you can use to describe the weather in your hometown.

Step 2: Open your essay with the name and location of your hometown (country, state, and city or town, in that order). Describe the seasons in your hometown, including whether it's relatively cold or warm, generally sunny or cloudy, whether it snows or rains and, if so, how much (a lot or a little). What kind of clothing do most people wear? Which leisure activities are most popular in each season? Conclude with a statement of your overall feeling about the weather in your hometown.

Step 3: Have someone proofread your essay, highlighting phrases they recognize and understand.

Step 4: Edit and polish your essay before handing it in for feedback, assessment, or adding to your writing portfolio.

2.6 我居住的地方 Where I Live—我的家乡 My Hometown—Levels A and B

我的家乡

A

我的家乡在密西根州的一个小城，小城就在湖边，人口只有一万多，大部分都是白人。

小城的最主要的一条街叫做第二街。这条街很长，而且街的两边都可以免费停车。街上有很多小商店，主要是卖本地的特产，比如Sweetland巧克力店的巧克力都是手工制作的。巧克力店旁边的冰淇淋店里也有好几种别的地方买不到的冰淇淋，而且这家店里的柜台、餐桌、座椅都是五十年代的。

小城里最古老的电影院就在这条街的最南边，这家电影院已经有70年的历史了。

图书馆在这条街的最北边。我上小学的时候，每个星期六的早上我都会到图书馆去借书。

除了各种各样的各有特色的小商店以外，这条街上还有很多长椅，这些椅子都被城里的居民自己油漆成不同的颜色和图案。椅子的两边也种了很多不同的颜色的花，春天和夏天的时候，花开了，把街道装点得很美丽。圣诞节的时候，整条街都挂起了彩灯，很有过节的气氛。

生词与短语 Words and Phrases 2.6 A

密西根	*Mìxīgēn*	Michigan
州	*zhōu*	state
大部分	*dàbùfen*	the majority
主要	*zhǔyào*	main; principal
免费	*miǎnfèi*	free of charge
停车	*tíngchē*	park
商店	*shāngdiàn*	store
本地	*běndì*	local
特产	*tèchǎn*	special local product
巧克力	*qiǎokèlì*	chocolate(s)
手工制作	*shǒugōng zhìzuò*	handmade
冰淇淋	*bīngqílín* (often pronounced *bīngqilíng*)	ice cream
柜台	*guìtái*	counter
餐桌	*cānzhuō*	dining table(s)
座椅	*zuòyǐ*	seat
五十年代	*wǔshí niándài*	the 50s (1950s)
古老	*gǔlǎo*	ancient; very old
各种各样的	*gèzhǒng gèyàngde*	every kind of
特色	*tèsè*	special; characteristic
长椅	*chángyǐ*	bench
居民	*jūmín*	residents; inhabitants
油漆	*yóuqī*	to paint
不同	*bùtóng*	not the same
图案	*tú-àn*	pattern; design
街道	*jiēdào*	street; neighborhood
装点	*zhuāngdiǎn*	decorate; dress up
圣诞节	*Shèndànjié*	Christmas
挂起	*guàqǐ*	hang up

生词与短语 Words and Phrases 2.6 A

彩灯	*cǎidēng*	colored lights
过节	*guòjié*	celebrate a holiday
气氛	*qìfēn*	atmosphere

2.6 Exercise 1—Reading Check

Reread the model text on the facing page and answer the following questions about the writer's hometown.

- Where is the writer's hometown located?
- What special sweet treats can you buy there?
- Name two buildings that are mentioned in the essay.
- Why are the benches in the town especially interesting?

注 Notes

1. Given the multiethnic nature of American society, it seems appropriate to introduce terms in Chinese for the largest ethnic groups in the United States.
   Caucasian 白人 *báirén*
   African AmAfrican American 非裔 fēiyì (used by Chinese Americans; 非洲裔人 is used in China as the formal term; the term 黑人 hēirén is still used in daily speech by ordinary people in China, since the term "Black people" does not have the history of racial discrimination it conveys in the U.S.)
   Hispanic American/Latino 拉丁美洲裔 *Lādīng Měizhōuyì*
   Mexican American 墨西哥裔 *Mòxīgēyì*
   Asian Americans 亚裔 *Yàyì* (the term *dōngfāngrén*, or "Orientals," should not be used to refer to Asian Americans)
2. The title of any movie, book, article should be bracketed by the Chinese punctuation sign 《》 (called书名号), rather than underlined or italicized as it is in English. For example, *U.S. News* should be written 《美国新闻》. Do not use underline or italics or other types of brackets such as angled brackets (< >)or square brackets ([ ].)

生词与短语 Words and Phrases 2.6 B

加州	*Jiāzhōu*	California
镇	*zhèn*	town
亚洲	*Yàzhōu*	Asia
方面	*fāngmiàn*	aspect(s); respect(s)
影响	*yǐngxiǎng*	influence
位于	*wèiyú*	be located in; be situated in
特别	*tèbié*	special
发现	*fāxiàn*	discover
季节	*jìjié*	season
据	*jù*	according to
报道	*bàodào*	report
全	*quán*	entire
排名	*páimíng*	(names) listed (in order by rank)
建议	*jiànyì*	suggest; recommend
一流	*yīliú*	first-class
却	*què*	however; actually (contrary to expectation)
图书	*túshū*	books (including some with pictures)
特别是	*tèbié shì*	especially
植物	*zhíwù*	plants
举办	*jǔbàn*	conduct; put on
音乐会	*yīnyuèhuì*	concerts
古典音乐	*gǔdiǎn yīnyuè*	classical music
流行音乐	*liúxíng yīnyuè*	popular music
购物中心	*gòuwù zhōngxīn*	shopping center; mall
名牌	*míngpái*	brand name

B

我可爱的家乡

我的家乡在加州的南部，是一个小镇，只有四万多人。因为百分之五十二以上的人口是亚洲人，所以我的家乡在很多方面都有亚洲文化的影响。

因为我的家乡位于南加州，天气特别好，差不多天天都是晴天。我到波士顿上大学以后才发现别的地方真的有春夏秋冬四个季节，而我的家乡只有春夏两个季节。除了天气很好以外，我的家乡也有非常好的学校。据《美国新闻》报道，我的高中在全加州排名第二。

如果你来我的小镇，我建议你到我们的图书馆去看看，因为我们的图书馆是一流的，虽然我们镇只有四万多人，我们的图书馆却有四十多万本图书。我们镇也有三十多个大大小小的公园，特别是湖边公园，非常漂亮，而且有一个很有名的“东方花园”，里边有很多美国没有的亚洲植物。夏天的时候，每个周末公园都会举办音乐会，有古典音乐，也有流行音乐。

我们的小镇也有一个非常大的购物中心，世界上最有名的名牌商店在那里都能找到。

B

购物中心的附近是一个非常繁华的地区，有各种各样的美食商店和餐馆。因为我们的小镇有很多不同的亚洲移民，有从中国来的、韩国来的，也有不少泰国人、菲律宾人、印度人，所以我们这里的食品都很地道，非常好吃而且价格也不贵。如果你来，千万不要忘了尝一尝正宗的中国小笼蒸包。

生词与短语 Words and Phrases 2.6 B

附近	*fùjìn*	vicinity; nearby area
繁华	*fánhuá*	thriving; bustling
地区	*dìqū*	area; district
美食	*měishí*	gourmet food
移民	*yímín*	immigrant(s)
泰国	*Tàiguó*	Thailand
菲律宾	*Fēilǜbīn*	Philippines
食品	*shípǐn*	foods
地道	*dìdào*	genuine; authentic
价格	*jiàgé*	price
千万	*qiānwàn*	by all means; definitely (almost always followed by 不 or 别 to mean "definitely don't . . .")
尝	*cháng*	to taste
正宗	*zhèngzōng*	authentic
小笼蒸包	*xiǎolóngzhēngbāo*	small dumplings cooked in a bamboo steamer

2.6 Exercise 2—Reading Check

Read the following statements about the above text. Underline where they appear in the text. Put a plus sign next to statements that are also true of your hometown.

_____ The town has forty thousand residents.

_____ There is a large Asian population in the town.

_____ The weather is usually sunny there.

_____ The library in the town is especially good.

_____ One of the parks in the town hosts summer concerts.

_____ There is a large shopping center in the town.

_____ Food served in the Asian restaurants in the town is very authentic.

2.6 Exercise 3—What Are the Highlights of Your Hometown?

Place a check in the boxes of places that you might highlight in your essay about your own hometown.

- ☐ 购物中心 *gòuwù zhōngxīn* shopping center; mall
- ☐ 停车 *tíngchē* park a car
- ☐ 商店 *shāngdiàn* store
- ☐ 湖 *hú* lake
- ☐ 河 *hé* river
- ☐ 电影院 *diànyǐngyuàn* movie theater
- ☐ 图书馆 *túshūguǎn* library
- ☐ 餐馆 *cānguǎn* restaurant
- ☐ 博物馆 *bówùguǎn* museum
- ☐ 大学 *dàxué* university
- ☐ 中学 *zhōngxué* high school

2.6 Exercise 4—Writing about Your Hometown—Drafting

Paragraph 1: Give the location (country, state, and city or town) and the approximate population of your hometown.

Paragraph 2: Describe the weather in your hometown in all four seasons, and your feelings about the weather there. Refer to Section 2.5 for words and phrases related to weather.

Paragraph 3: Describe the notable characteristics of your hometown, including any major landmarks and important buildings, as well as its scenic features (e.g., lakes, rivers, mountains, parks).

Paragraph 4: Mention the special things your town offers and what, if anything, it lacks in your opinion. Conclude with your feelings about your hometown.

Writing about Your Own Hometown

Step 1: Compose your essay, following the paragraph structure in the sample texts and using the key words and phrases you identified for each section.

Step 2: Have someone proofread your essay, highlighting phrases that they immediately recognize and understand.

Step 3: Edit and polish your essay before handing it in for feedback, assessment, or adding to your writing portfolio.

2.7 我居住的地方 Where I Live 校园生活 Campus Life—我的专业 My Major—Levels A and B

生词与短语 Words and Phrases 2.7 A

专业	*zhuānyè*	major field of study
选	*xuǎn*	choose; select
写起来	*xiěqǐlái*	upon writing
毕业	*bìyè*	graduate
研究生院	*yánjiūshēngyuàn*	graduate school (only used in mainland China)
为 . . . . . 工作	*wèi . . . gōngzuò*	work for . . .
学好	*xuéhǎo*	learn (successfully)
机会	*jīhuì*	chance; opportunity
比如说	*bǐrú shuō*	for example
政府	*zhèngfǔ*	government

2.7 Exercise 1—Reading Check

Reread the model text on this page and explain the writer's rationale for choosing to study Chinese.

- Why did the writer choose Chinese in high school?
- Why does the writer like learning Chinese?
- Why did the writer choose Chinese as a major in college?

A

我的专业

我的专业是中文。我从小就喜欢学外语，初中的时候我学了几年的西班牙文。上了高中就听说有中文课，因为中国是很重要的国家，而且我也有个朋友是从中国来的，所以我决定选中文课。中文比西班牙文有意思，因为汉字非常漂亮，写起来也很好玩。

我也很喜欢我的中文老师。他是从北京来的，教书教得很好，所以我一共上了三年的中文课。

上大学的时候我就决定我的专业应当是中文。我毕业以后打算先到中国去教几年的英文，然后或者上研究生院或者为一家国际公司工作。我知道如果我学好中文，就会有更多更好的工作机会。比如说：我不但可以做买卖，也可以为美国政府工作。当然如果我上研究生院我还可以在高中或者在大学教中文、中国历史，等等。我还不知道我将来会做什么工作，但是我知道学中文一定能帮助我找到有意思的工作。

两个专业

B

我有两个专业。对我来说，选择这两个专业有必然性，也有偶然性。

我的第一个专业是电脑科学，这个选择来得很自然，因为我的父母在我还很小的时候就买了一台电脑，我整天用那台电脑玩，很快就用得非常熟练了。高中那几年，我的朋友们都很精通电脑，我们经常在一起讨论的话题都是关于电脑，所以上大学前，我就已经知道我会选电脑作为我的专业。

我的另一个专业是汉语，这却是事出偶然。我在大学的第一个学期本来选了一门数学课，但是我很快发现这门课对我来说太难了，我决定退课，但是我必须再选一门别的课。我跟我的指导教授和汉语教授商量了以后，决定选学汉语。很快我就发现我很喜欢学汉语，想继续学下去，于是我就决定把汉语当做我的第二个专业。

生词与短语 Words and Phrases 2.7 B

选择	*xuǎnzé*	choose; select (often shortened to 选)
必然性	*bìránxìng*	inevitability
偶然性	*ǒuránxìng*	by chance
自然	*zìrán*	natural
整天	*zhěngtiān*	the whole day; all day long
熟练	*shúliàn*	skilled; proficient
精通	*jīngtōng*	be proficient in; have a command of
讨论	*tǎolùn*	discuss
话题	*huàtí*	topic or subject of conversation
关于	*guānyú*	concerning; about
作为	*zuòwéi*	take as; regard as
却	*què*	however; actually (contrary to expectation)
事出偶然	*shì chū ǒurán*	something that happened by chance
发现	*fāxiàn*	discover
退课	*tuìkè*	withdraw from a course
指导教授	*zhǐdǎo jiàoshòu*	adviser; advising professor
商量	*shāngliang*	to talk over
继续	*jìxù*	continue
于是	*yúshì*	consequently; thereupon
把 ..... 当做	*bǎ . . . dāngzuò*	take/treat . . . as . . .

2.7 Exercise 2—College Subjects

Circle the subject(s) you are planning to major in. Put a check mark in the box next to the subjects you like and an X next to the subjects you don't. Add any subjects you need that aren't on the list. Think about the reasons you do and don't like particular subjects.

- 汉语 — *Hànyǔ* — Chinese
  (汉语 is technically the spoken language and 中文 the written language, but many Chinese speakers use them synonymously)
- 西班牙语 — *Xībānyáyǔ* — Spanish
- 英语 — *Yīngyǔ* — English
- 历史 — *lìshǐ* — history
- 经济学 — *jīngjìxué* — economics
- 计算机科学 — *jìsuànjī kēxué* — computer science
- 数学 — *shùxué* — mathematics
- 化学 — *huàxué* — chemistry
- （艺术家的）工作室艺术 — *(yìshùjiā de) gōngzuòshì yìshù* — studio art
- 心理学 — *xīnlǐxué* — psychology
- 音乐 — *yīnyuè* — music
- 生物学 — *shēngwùxué* — biology
- 社会学 — *shèhuìxué* — sociology
- 哲学 — *zhéxué* — philosophy

2.7 Exercise 3—Writing about Your Own Major—Drafting

Begin drafting an essay about your own major by brainstorming the following topics. Draw on the words and phrases presented in this section, as well as the model text(s).

Major: State your major(s) and give the reason(s) you chose it (them).

Courses: Mention some of the specific courses you need to take for your major(s), and what you find interesting or boring, difficult or easy, about those courses.

Career goals: Describe your career goals related to your major(s) and how you plan to use the acquired knowledge and skills in the future.

Writing about Your Own Major

Step 1: Compose your essay, drawing on the topics above for the individual paragraphs and using the key words and phrases you identified for each section, as well as the sample texts as models.

Step 2: Have someone proofread your essay, highlighting phrases that they immediately recognize and understand.

Step 3: Edit and polish your essay before handing it in for feedback, assessment, or adding to your writing portfolio.

2.8 日常生活 Daily Life—我的衣服 My Wardrobe—Levels A and B

生词与短语 Words and Phrases 2.8 A

校外	*xiàowài*	outside of school; off campus
打工	*dǎgōng*	work (for someone at a manual labor job, usually just part-time and temporary)
赚	*zhuàn*	earn; make (money)
内裤	*nèikù*	underpants; underwear
皮鞋	*píxié*	leather shoes
意大利	*Yìdàlì*	Italy; Italian
休闲	*xiūxián*	leisure
浅	*qiǎn*	light (in color)
褐色	*hèsè*	brown
另一件	*lìng yíjiàn*	an additional one; still another
球鞋	*qiúxié*	tennis shoes; sneakers
平常的时候	*píngchángde shíhou*	generally; usually

2.8 Exercise 1—Vocab Grab

Write down items of clothing presented in the model(s) that you can use in describing your own wardrobe.

A

我的衣服

我除了上大学以外还在校外打工，因为我需要赚一点买书的钱，当然，我也会用这些钱买衣服，所以我的衣服大概比别的二十岁的男的多一点儿。我一共有六件衬衫：三件是白色的、两件是黑色的、一件是深蓝色的。我也有四条黑色的裤子。我当然也有很多条内裤和很多双袜子。我还有一双很贵的黑色的皮鞋，那是在意大利做的，我工作的时候就会穿。冬天的时候我会穿一件黑色的大衣。

我也有休闲的衣服，比如说我有五件T-恤衫、两条浅蓝色的牛仔裤、三条咖啡色的短裤和一件浅褐色的夹克。我也有两件毛衣，一件是红色的，另一件是灰色的。我还有一双白色的球鞋。我夏天平常的时候会穿T-恤衫和短裤，冬天穿毛衣、牛仔裤和夹克。

B

说说穿衣

我有很多衣服，所以我大概需要一点时间来形容。

我有十件衬衫：两件是深蓝色的、三件是浅蓝色的、一件是粉色的、一件是灰色的、一件是白色的、一件是黑红色条纹的、一件是紫灰色条纹的。如果我只需要去上课，我就会换穿这些衬衫。

但是如果我需要去工作，我就会穿连衣裙，因为我的老板要求我们必须穿正式的衣服上班。我有三条连衣裙：一条是绿色的、一条是红色的、一条是黄色的，不过我很少穿这条黄色的，因为我觉得这个颜色对我的肤色不太适合。

有时候我也会穿短裙去上课。我有四条短裙：两条是黑色的、一条是有金色的小花的黑裙子，但我最喜欢的是一条有浅紫色的花朵图案的。我穿短裙的时候就会配穿短袖衫，我有好几件短袖的上衣，有蓝色的、白色的、粉色的，等等。

我有两双白色球鞋，我跑步的时候就会穿。三双凉鞋是天气热的时候穿短裙外出的时候穿的，六双高跟鞋是穿连衣裙去工作的时候穿的。

我当然也有两条牛仔裤，那是跟朋友出去看电影的时候穿的。

生词与短语 Words and Phrases 2.8 B

形容	*xíngróng*	describe
条纹	*tiáowén*	stripes
换穿	*huàn chuān*	vary what you wear from day to day
老板	*lǎobǎn*	boss
要求	*yāoqiú*	require; demand
正式	*zhèngshì*	formal
上班	*shàngbān*	go to work
肤色	*fūsè*	skin color
对 . . . . . . 适合	*duì . . . shìhé*	suitable for . . .
花朵图案	*huāduǒ túàn*	floral pattern
配穿	*pèichuān*	to match
短袖衫	*duǎnxiùshān*	short-sleeved shirt or blouse
外出	*wàichū*	go out
高跟鞋	*gāogēnxié*	high heels

Writing about Your Own Wardrobe

Step 1: Compose your essay, drawing on vocabulary items you noted down in 2.8 Exercise 1 and the model text(s).

- **Formal wear:** Describe in detail what clothes you wear in more formal situations, such as work, attending class, going out, attending worship, and parties. Give the number and color of types of tops, pants and/or skirts and dresses, coats, and shoes in your wardrobe.
- **Leisure wear:** Do the same for the clothing you wear for leisure activities, being sure to include the number and color of T-shirts, shorts, jackets, and sneakers or running shoes in your wardrobe.

Step 2: Proofread, edit, and polish your essay, following the process you have previously used.

2.9 日常生活 Daily Life—我的日程表 My Schedule—Levels A and B

生词与短语 Words and Phrases 2.9 A

日程表	*rìchéngbiǎo*	daily schedule
总是	*zǒngshì*	always
困	*kùn*	sleepy; tired

2.9 Exercise 1—Reading Check

Read the model text on this page and fill in the activities mentioned by the writer.

8:00 a.m. __________

9:00 a.m. __________

10:00 a.m. __________

11:00 a.m. __________

12:00 p.m. __________

2:00 p.m. __________

5:00 p.m. __________

8:00 p.m. __________

12:30 a.m. __________

A

我的日程表

我念大学二年级。我平常早上八点钟起床，我很少吃早饭。这个学期我一共上四门课。星期一、三、五从早上九点钟到九点五十分我上英文文学的课。星期一到星期五上午十点钟到十点五十分我有中文课。那是我最喜欢的课，因为中文很有意思，再说我们的老师真是一个有趣的人。星期二和星期四从上午十一点钟到中午十二点半我上中国历史课。星期一、三、五我从中午十二点到下午一点在学生餐厅跟我的朋友一起吃午饭。星期二和星期四我十二点半到下午一点半自己在餐厅吃午饭。星期三从下午两点到四点半我有生物学的课。

每个星期我不但要上十二个小时的课，也需要工作十四个钟头。每天从下午五点到晚上七点在餐厅工作。除了星期天以外我每天晚上从八点到十点在图书馆里念书。我平常夜里十二点半睡觉。我总是睡七个到七个半小时的觉，但是我往往还是觉得很困。

B

一周的作息时间表

我是一个大三的学生，我这个学期非常忙碌。我选了五门课，一共16个学分。我的专业是儿童教育，所以我选的课程多半都跟儿童教育有关。

我每周一、三上午8:00到9:00上一节教育课，10:00到11:00上一节儿童阅读课。每周一、三、五下午1:30到2:30上一节儿童早期教育课。每周二、四下午2:30到3:30上一节语言学课。每周三下午3:30到4:30上一节儿童心理学课。

每周五的早上6:00我就得起床，因为我7:30就要到当地的一个小学去做实习，在那所小学我整整一个上午给老师当助教。下午回到大学上完课后我就会去学校的图书馆工作四个小时。周末的时候我也会每天在大学的学生餐厅工作两个小时。

因为白天时间紧，所以晚上是我做功课的时间。我每天大概要花四、五个小时做作业和预习第二天的课。

有时间的时候，我会和朋友们聊天，一起看轻松搞笑的电视节目来放松一下。

生词与短语 Words and Phrases 2.9 B

一周	*yìzhōu*	one week (shorthand term in written language)
作息时间表	*zuòxī shíjiānbiǎo*	daily work and rest (play) schedule
忙碌	*mánglù*	busy
学分	*xuéfēn*	credits (in school)
儿童教育	*értóng jiàoyù*	elementary education
课程	*kèchéng*	classes; curriculum
多半	*duōbàn*	most
跟……有关	*gēn . . . yǒuguān*	related to
节	*jié*	measure word for class periods
阅读	*yuèdú*	read
早期	*zǎoqī*	early stage
语言学	*yǔyánxué*	linguistics
心理学	*xīnlǐxué*	psychology
实习	*shíxí*	practicum; practical training
所	*suǒ*	measure word for buildings, etc.
整整	*zhěngzhěng*	entire; whole
当	*dāng*	to serve as
助教	*zhùjiào*	teaching assistant
紧	*jǐn*	tight; pressing
预习	*yùxí*	study lessons before class
轻松	*qīngsōng*	lighthearted; relaxed
搞笑	*gǎoxiào*	funny; hilarious
放松	*fàngsōng*	relax

2.9 Exercise 2—Brainstorming Your Schedule

Fill in the table below with notes (in Chinese) about your own schedule.

	During the Week	Weekend
Morning		
Afternoon		
Evening		

注 Notes

These days 九点钟到九点五十分 would more likely be written as 9点到 9点50分 or even 9:00到 9:50. But the first model text shows that it is not wrong to continue to use Chinese characters to represent numbers.

Writing about Your Own Class and Work Schedule

Step 1: Compose your essay, drawing on the information you summarized in the table at left. Address the following topics:

- Give your year in school and how many classes you're taking. Comment on how busy you feel in general, based on the level of difficulty and demands of your courses.
- Describe what days and times you have each of your classes.
- Mention when you get up and go to bed on weekdays and weekends.
- If you have a job, describe where you work and what days and times you're on the job.

Step 2: Have someone proofread your essay, highlighting phrases that they immediately recognize and understand.

Step 3: Edit and polish your essay before handing it in for feedback, assessment, or adding to your writing portfolio.

第三章 Accounts of Personal Experiences 描写个人经历 3

3.1 五花八门的人生阅历 Various Life Experiences—我的童年 My Childhood—Level A

生词与短语 Words and Phrases 3.1 A

童年	*tóngnián*	childhood
芝加哥	*Zhījiāgē*	Chicago
所	*suǒ*	measure word for buildings
直到……为止	*zhídào . . . wéi zhǐ*	right up until . . .
印地安纳州	*Yìndìānnà zhōu*	(state of) Indiana
镇	*zhèn*	town
唯一	*wéiyī*	only one; sole
北郊	*běijiāo*	northern suburbs
富裕	*fùyù*	wealthy; well-to-do
地区	*dìqū*	area; region
……之一	*zhī yī*	one of the . . .
只是	*zhǐshì*	only
推销员	*tuīxiāoyuán*	sales representative; salesperson
家庭主妇	*jiātíng zhǔfù*	housewife
受到	*shòudào*	receive (in an abstract sense)

A

我的童年

我是在芝加哥的一所医院里出生的，但是直到我5岁为止我的家是在印地安纳州的一个小镇里。

我出生的时候我爸爸40岁了，我妈妈32岁了。我是我父母的第一个孩子，我也是他们唯一的儿子，我妹妹在我出生后的一年半以后出生了。

我5岁的时候我父母搬到芝加哥的北郊，那是美国最富裕的地区之一，所以那里的学校也是美国最好的学校之一，虽然我的父亲只是一个推销员，我的妈妈是一个家庭主妇，但是为了我和我的妹妹能受到最好的教育，他们把家搬到这个富裕地区里的一条很普通的小街上。

(Continues on the next page.)

A

(我的童年 *continued*)

我家附近有一块空地，那是我和邻居小孩子们的玩耍天堂，我们每天在那里打棒球、玩美式足球、篮球。但是我也很喜欢阅读，在学校我也是一个很好的学生。我从10岁起开始学习拉小提琴。我的小提琴老师是一个很有名的小提琴家，她也曾经是我妈妈的小提琴老师，在她的教育下，我很快便成为我们学校的最好的小提琴手，但每当我偷懒没有努力练习小提琴时，她立刻就能听出来，她总是说：少看点电视，多拉点提琴！

我上高中以后，我每天晚上都有三、四个小时的作业，我没有那么多时间跟我的朋友们玩儿了，但是我还是在学校的交响乐团拉小提琴，而且我从初中一年级就开始学习西班牙文，直到高中一共学了6年，我想我就是从那时候开始爱上学习外语了。

生词与短语 Words and Phrases 3.1 A (*continued*)

附近	*fùjìn*	vicinity; neighborhood
空地	*kòngdì*	vacant lot
邻居	*línjū*	neighbors
玩耍	*wánshuǎ*	play; have fun
天堂	*tiāntáng*	heaven
阅读	*yuèdú*	read
拉小提琴	*lā xiǎotíqín*	play the violin
小提琴家	*xiǎotíqínjiā*	master violinist
小提琴手	*xiǎotíqínshǒu*	violinist
偷懒	*tōulǎn*	be lazy; loaf off
努力	*nǔlì*	try hard; make a great effort
上	*shàng*	attend
交响乐团	*jiāoxiǎngyuètuán*	symphony orchestra
初中	*chūzhōng*	middle school; junior high
爱上	*àishàng*	fall in love with

3.1 Exercise 1—Reading Check

- How many members are there in this family?
- What jobs are mentioned?
- Why did the family move to Chicago?
- What hobbies are mentioned?

3.1 Exercise 2—Vocab Grab

How do you say . . . ?

- “when I was 5”
- “up until I was 5”
- “(ever) since I was 10 years old”
- “after I was in high school”

注 Notes

1. **每当……时 (的时候), 就……**
   měidāng . . . shí (de shíhou), jiù . . .
   Every time, . . . then . . .

   每当过中国新年**时**，我**就**更加想念我的家人。
   Měidāng guò Zhōngguó xīnnián shí, wǒ jiù gèngjiā xiǎngniàn wǒde jiārén.
   Every time we celebrate the Chinese New Year, I miss my family even more.

   在美国留学的那四年里，**每当**我在生活上有问题**时**，我**就**会请我的美国朋友帮助我。
   Zài Měiguó liúxué de nà sìnián lǐ, měidāng wǒ zài shēnghuóshàng yǒu wèntí shí, wǒ jiù huì qǐng wǒde Měiguó péngyou bāngzhù wǒ.
   During those four years that I was studying in the U.S. as a foreign student, every time I had a problem in my life there, I'd ask my American friends to help me.

2. 少 + verb 一点/点 + object
   to [verb] a bit less

   少看(一)点电视。
   Shǎo kàn (yì)diǎn diànshì.
   Watch less TV.

   炒菜请少放(一)点盐。
   Chǎo cài qǐng shǎo fàng (yì)diǎn yán.
   When you cook (stir-fry), please put in less salt.

3. 多 + verb 一点/点 + object
   to ____ a bit more

   多吃一点水果，少吃一点油炸的东西。
   Duō chī yìdiǎn shuǐguǒ, shǎo chī yìdiǎn yóuzhá de dōngxi.
   Eat more fruit and fewer deep-fried foods.

   多吃一点青菜，少吃一点盐。
   Duō chī yìdiǎn qīngcài, shǎo chī yìdiǎn yán.
   Eat more green vegetables and less salt.

3.1 五花八门的人生阅历 Various Life Experiences—我的童年 My Childhood—Level B

B

欢乐的童年

我觉得我的童年是开心和幸福的。因为我是一个独生子女，我的父母非常疼爱我。记得小时候我有一个芭比娃娃，我给她起名叫"公主"，我非常想给我的"公主"找一个王子，可是那时在北京买不到王子，我的爸爸四处给我找王子，最后在他出国出差到西班牙的时候在机场给我买到了王子！我高兴极了！

小时候最开心的事是和小伙伴儿们一起玩。我们在院子里打水枪、在操场上跳橡皮筋、在同学的家里玩捉迷藏、在家里玩电子游戏……

小学的时候也看了很多有趣的童话故事，比如一年级时看了格林童话、安徒生童话；二、三年级时看了纽伯瑞系列儿童获奖丛书；四、五年级时又看了哈利波特，都留下了深刻印象。

我非常怀念小时候的时光，没有烦恼、没有忧虑，只有欢乐和幸福。

生词与短语 Words and Phrases 3.1 B

欢乐	*huānlè*	joy; happiness
童年	*tóngnián*	childhood
开心	*kāixīn*	happy
幸福	*xìngfú*	fortunate; blessed
独生子女	*dúshēng zǐnǚ*	only child, either male or female
疼爱	*téng-ài*	love dearly; dote on
芭比娃娃	*Bābǐ wáwa*	Barbie doll
公主	*gōngzhǔ*	princess
王子	*wángzǐ*	prince
四处	*sìchù*	all directions; everywhere
伙伴儿们	*huǒbànrmen*	companions; buddies
水枪	*shuǐqiāng*	squirt guns; water pistols
跳橡皮筋	*tiào xiàngpíjīn*	jumping game with elastic bands
捉迷藏	*zhuōmícáng*	hide-and-seek
电子游戏	*diànzǐ yóuxì*	video games
童话故事	*tónghuà gùshi*	children's stories; fairy tales
时	*shí*	short for 时候 in writing
格林	*Gélín*	Grimm (Brothers)
安徒生	*Āntúshēng*	(Hans Christian) Andersen
纽伯瑞	*Niǔbóruì*	Newbery
系列	*xìliè*	series
获奖	*huòjiǎng*	prize-winning
丛书	*cóngshū*	a series of books; collection
哈利波特	*Hālìbōtè*	Harry Potter
留下……印象	*liúxià . . . yìnxiàng*	leave a . . . impression
深刻	*shēnkè*	deep; profound
怀念	*huáiniàn*	cherish the memory of
时光	*shíguāng*	time; years
烦恼	*fánnǎo*	be worried; troubled
忧虑	*yōulǜ*	anxious; concerned

注 Notes

4. 给……起名　*gěi . . . qǐmíng*
   to give ____ a name; to name somebody or something

   例句 **Example Sentences**

   我的中文老师**给**我**起**了一个很好听的中文名字。
   Wǒde zhōngwén lǎoshī gěi wǒ qǐle yíge hěn hǎotīngde zhōngwén míngzi.
   My Chinese teacher gave me a nice-sounding Chinese name.

   我**给**我的小猫**起**了一个很有意思的名字。
   Wǒ gěi wǒde xiǎomāo qǐle yíge hěn yǒuyìside míngzi.
   I gave my kitten a very interesting name.

5. 给……找　*gěi . . . zhǎo*　look (for something) for somebody

   例句 **Example Sentences**

   妈妈要出门，却找不到她的钥匙，她对我说："快！
   给我**找找**钥匙！"
   Māma yào chūmén, què zhǎobúdào tāde yàoshi, tā duì wǒ shuō: "Kuài! Gěi wǒ zhǎozhao yàoshi!"
   (When) Mom was about to leave the house, but couldn't find her keys, she said to me: "Quick! Find my keys for me!"

   我请他上网**给**我爸爸**找**一个合适的礼物。
   Wǒ qǐng tā shàngwǎng gěi wǒ bàba zhǎo yíge héshìde lǐwù.
   I asked him to get online for me and find a suitable present for my father.

6. The Chinese have adopted the English ellipsis (. . .). But instead of three dots, the Chinese use six dots, and so in this book we also use six dots for ellipsis in sentences or phrases.

3.1 Exercise 3—Writing about Your Childhood—Text Building

Use the text builder to plan out the draft of your essay one paragraph at a time.

Plan your paragraphs:	Grab key vocab and phrases from the three model essays above describing "My Childhood" for these targeted items in each paragraph:
1. • Your hometown: What type of place is it? • Your family: How old were your parents when you were born? How old are your siblings compared to you (e.g., 我的哥哥比我大两岁; My brother is two years older than me)?	
2. Describe what you liked to do for fun as a child and with whom you played.	
3. Describe how you felt about school. What did you like or dislike? What were your favorite and least favorite subjects?	
4. Describe how you feel in general about your childhood—was it happy, unhappy, fun, etc.	

Writing about Your childhood

Step 1: Compose your essay using your key words and phrases from the text builder in 3.1 Exercise 3, as well as the sample texts as models.

Step 2: Have someone proofread your essay, highlighting phrases that they immediately recognize and understand. Double check any items you are unsure of.

Step 3: Edit and polish your essay before handing it in for feedback, assessment, or adding to your writing portfolio.

3.2 五花八门的人生阅历 Various Life Experiences—我最喜欢的节日 My Favorite Holiday—Levels A and B

A

我最喜欢的节日

我最喜欢的节日是圣诞节，因为圣诞节的时候我可以跟我最爱的人们在一起，吃好吃的圣诞火腿，特别是我有机会给我最爱的人礼物。

我一般会花很多时间来考虑我应该给他们什么礼物。对我来说，与我最亲近的人，我一般会为他们精心地画画或者做首饰给他们。我觉得亲手制作的礼物最能表现你对他们的感激。虽然亲手制作礼物会让我花很多的时间，但我在制作礼物的过程中很快乐，特别是到了圣诞节那天时，当我看到人们打开我给他们的礼物时的满脸的笑容时，就觉得很值得花那么多的时间给他们制作礼物。

圣诞节是亲朋好友们团聚的一天，也是带给我的亲朋好友们喜悦的一天，那是为什么我最喜欢圣诞节。

生词与短语 Words and Phrases 3.2 A

节日	*jiérì*	holiday; festival
圣诞节	*Shèngdànjié*	Christmas
火腿	*huǒtuǐ*	ham
特别是	*tèbié shì*	especially
机会	*jīhuì*	opportunity; chance
礼物	*lǐwù*	present; gift
一般	*yìbān*	in general; for the most part
考虑	*kǎolǜ*	consider; think over
与……亲近	*yǔ . . . qīnjìn*	be close with . . .
精心地	*jīngxīnde*	meticulously; elaborately
首饰	*shǒushi*	jewelry
亲手制作	*qīnshǒu zhìzuò*	made with one's own hands
表现	*biǎoxiàn*	express; show
感激	*gǎnjī*	gratitude
让……花时间	*ràng . . . huā shíjiān*	make . . . spend time
过程中	*guòchéng zhōng*	in the process
时	*shí*	short for 时候 in writing
满脸	*mǎn liǎn*	across one's whole face
笑容	*xiàoróng*	smiling expression; smile
值得	*zhídé*	be worth it
亲朋好友们	*qīnpéng hǎoyǒumen*	friends and family
团聚	*tuánjù*	reunite
喜悦	*xǐyuè*	happy; joyous

3.2 Exercise 1—Vocab Grab

Grab three to five phrases from the model texts that you can adapt to use in your own description of a favorite holiday.

生词与短语 Words and Phrases 3.2 B

过节	*guòjié*	celebrate a holiday
当中	*dāngzhōng*	among
团聚	*tuánjù*	reunite
庆祝	*qìngzhù*	celebrate
最最	*zuìzuì*	the utmost (only used in colloquial speech)
前夜	*qiányè*	the night before
事实上	*shìshíshàng*	in fact
亲戚	*qīnqi*	relatives
到达	*dàodá*	arrive
到齐	*dàoqí*	to be all present
批	*pī*	a batch (measure word)
……之一	*zhī yī*	one of the . . .
随着	*suízhe*	along with
表哥表姐	*biǎogē biǎojiě*	older male and female cousins on the mother's side of the family
属于	*shǔyú*	belong to; be part of
急切	*jíqiè*	eager; impatient
撕开	*sīkāi*	tear open
包装纸	*bāozhuāngzhǐ*	wrapping paper
发现	*fāxiàn*	discover
得到	*dédào*	get; receive
期待	*qīdài*	expect; look forward to
欢呼	*huānhū*	cheer
兴奋	*xīngfèn*	get excited
渴望	*kěwàng*	thirst for sth.
现金	*xiànjīn*	cash
甜点	*tiándiǎn*	dessert
唯一	*wéiyī*	the only
了解	*liǎojiě*	understand; acquaint oneself with
情况	*qíngkuàng*	situation
珍惜	*zhēnxī*	treasure; cherish
利用	*lìyòng*	make use of

B

最重要的节日

过节对我们家来说非常重要，一年当中，我们的大家庭常常会团聚在一起庆祝节日，但最最重要的是圣诞节的前夜的团聚。事实上，我的奶奶会花两个星期的时间来准备我们的圣诞节活动。

圣诞节前夜的那天下午，我们就会到我奶奶的家里。在别的亲戚到达之前，我会帮助奶奶做各种各样的菜，因为我们的大家庭有20多个人，所以我们得做很多很多菜。家人都到齐以后，我们就会吃饭。

吃完饭以后我们就会到客厅里去打开圣诞礼物。我们会先从最小的孩子开始，我以前也是最先一批打开礼物的孩子之一，但随着我慢慢地长大了，我的表哥表姐们也都有了他们自己的孩子，我现在属于第二批打开礼物的人了。看着表哥表姐们的小孩子们急切地撕开礼物的包装纸、发现他们得到了他们期待的礼物时的欢呼很好玩。当然，看别人得到他们想要的礼物让我高兴，但是我还是最兴奋我自己得到最想要的礼物。因为我是一个大学学生，我一般会渴望得到我最想要看的书或者是现金，因为那样我就可以和我的朋友们出去吃饭。

家人都打开了礼物以后，我们就会一边吃甜点一边聊天。这是为什么我最喜欢圣诞节前夜的家庭聚会，因为这是一年里唯一的机会我可以见到我们的大家庭的每一个人，了解他们在这一年里的情况。

我非常珍惜我每年都可以利用圣诞节这个节日和我的家人一起团聚。

3.2 Exercise 2—Reading Check

Check your comprehension of the models on the previous pages by answering the questions below.

Level A

1. Why is Christmas the writer's favorite holiday?

2. What types of gifts does the writer like to give close friends and family?

Level B

1. What role does the grandmother play in the holiday traditions?

2. What types of presents does the writer like to get and why?

3.2 Exercise 3—Vocab Grab

Skim through the model texts on describing a favorite holiday and highlight several phrases that you can use to describe your own holiday. Then, practice writing at least five of the most important ones that you chose below.

3.2 Exercise 4—Vocab Building

Research the words you need to describe foods, activities, and a tradition associated with your favorite holiday that you will write about. Take notes here and then check to make sure that your word choices are appropriate.

3.2 Exercise 5—Writing about Your Favorite Holiday—Drafting

Read through the models again and review Exercises 3 and 4 in this section. In the blue spaces below, draft a first sentence and then add some of the key phrases for each paragraph.

Paragraph 1: Mention your favorite holiday and the time of year it occurs. Describe what you and your family do to prepare to celebrate.

Paragraph 2: Describe how you celebrate and with whom. Include the special food(s) you enjoy and any family traditions such as presents, games, fasting, etc.

Paragraph 3: Describe some special activities that are part of your celebration, such as going to church, temple, or mosque; visiting friends or other family members, traveling, etc.

Paragraph 4: Conclude by presenting the reasons that this holiday is your favorite.

Writing about Your Favorite Holiday

Step 1: Following the model and using your vocabulary and phrases from above, draft your essay one paragraph at a time.

Step 2: Make a list (following the Words and Phrases style) of the specific vocabulary or phrases for your holiday that may be unfamiliar to other learners.

Step 3: Have someone read and respond to your essay by describing three things they learned about your holiday traditions.

3.3 五花八门的人生阅历 Various Life Experiences—我病了 An Illness—Level A

A

我病了

我上个星期病了。我的头疼死了，肚子也很不舒服。我的同屋说看起来我的病很严重，他觉得我应该去看病，所以我就去看了王大夫，她是我们的校医，大家都说她是很好的医生。

王大夫叫我在床上躺下做检查。我问她我得了什么病，厉害不厉害，我说我希望不必打针，因为我怕疼。王大夫说我病得不厉害，不用害怕。王大夫问我最近吃了什么东西、喝了什么东西。我告诉她前一天我到校外参加了一个聚会，吃了很多热狗、汉堡包、比萨饼、冰淇淋，也喝了很多啤酒。王大夫就说因为我吃了太多的垃圾食品，吃坏肚子了，所以肚子疼了，而且因为我喝醉了，所以头也疼了。她叫我以后要少吃垃圾食品，不要喝酒。她也劝告我要多运动，因为我太胖了。

我现在打算找别的医生！

注 Notes

1. If you want to say you are *very* sick, you can either say 我病得很厉害 or 我的病很严重. It is incorrect to say 我很病.

生词与短语 Words and Phrases 3.3 A

看起来	*kànqǐlái*	looks like
严重	*yánzhòng*	serious; critical
校医	*xiàoyī*	school physician
得……病	*dé . . . bìng*	contract a disease
厉害	*lìhai*	severe
不必	*búbì*	don't have to
打针	*dǎzhēn*	get a shot
害怕	*hàipà*	be afraid; scared
前一天	*qián yìtiān*	the day before (an event)
聚会	*jùhuì*	gathering; party
热狗	*règǒu*	hot dog
汉堡包	*hànbǎobāo*	hamburger
比萨饼	*bǐsàbǐng*	pizza
冰淇淋	*bīngqílín* (pronounced *bīngqílíng*, at least in the north)	ice cream
垃圾食品	*lājī shípǐn*	junk food
吃坏肚子	*chīhuài dùzi*	get an upset stomach from eating
喝醉	*hēzuì*	get drunk
劝告	*quàngào*	advise

3.3 Exercise 1—Vocab Grab

Review the model text, highlighting key characters or phrases that you might use to describe an illness or doctor appointment. Write a few of those in the blue box.

注 Notes

2. There are many ways to translate the English word *tell* into Chinese, depending on what you mean.

叫	*jiào*	tell someone to do something
告诉	*gàosu*	tell or inform someone of something
说	*shuō*	tell a story
讲	*jiǎng*	tell a story

- 叫 means "to tell someone to do something," if that person is someone in authority. Therefore,王大夫叫我在床上躺下 means "Dr. Wang told me to lie down on the bed."
- 告诉 means "to tell someone something" in the sense of informing them. 我告诉她前一天我到校外参加了一个聚会 means "I told her (informed her that) I took part in a gathering off-campus the day before."
- When you want to say "tell a story" in Chinese, you either say 说一个故事 (gùshi) or 讲 (jiǎng) 一个故事.

3. Similarly, there are several ways to translate the word *ask* into Chinese, depending on what you mean.

叫	*jiào*	to tell or ask someone to do something
问	*wèn*	to inquire; to ask a question
请	*qǐng*	to request; invite

In model text A, 王大夫叫我在床上躺下 could be translated as "Dr. Wang asked (told) me to lie down on the bed." But the sentence 我问她我得了什么病 translates as "I asked her (inquired) what illness I had contracted." In contrast, if you "ask" (request) someone to do a favor for you, or you "ask" (invite) someone to dinner, then you use the word 请.

生词与短语 Words and Phrases 3.3 B

嗓子	*sǎngzi*	throat
感冒	*gǎnmào*	have a cold
治	*zhì*	cure
开始	*kāishǐ*	begin; start
咳嗽	*késou*	cough
打喷嚏	*dǎ pēntì*	sneeze
浑身	*húnshēn*	from head to foot; all over
酸疼	*suānténg*	sore; soreness
药店	*yàodiàn*	pharmacy
阿司匹林	*Āsīpǐlín*	aspirin
管用	*guǎnyòng*	effective; useful
发烧	*fāshāo*	have a fever
发冷	*fālěng*	shiver
恶心	*ěxīn*	nauseous
吐	*tù*	vomit; throw up
赶紧	*gǎnjǐn*	without delay; immediately
病情	*bìngqíng*	patient's condition
消炎药	*xiāoyányào*	antibiotic
打……针	*dǎ . . . zhēn*	get a shot
退烧	*tuìshāo*	reduce fever
检查	*jiǎnchá*	examine
体温	*tǐwēn*	body temperature
流感	*liúgǎn*	flu (流感 is short for 流行性感冒 *liúxíngxìng gǎnmào)*
专治	*zhuānzhì*	used specifically for the treatment of
开……药	*kāi . . . yào*	write a prescription
尽量	*jìnliàng*	as much as possible
传染	*chuánrán*	infect

3.3 五花八门的人生阅历 Various Life Experiences—我病了 An Illness—Level B

B

我病得很厉害

今天早上一起床我就觉得头疼、嗓子疼，我想我大概是感冒了，就吃了两片治感冒的药就去上课了。但是到了中午我开始咳嗽、打喷嚏，而且浑身酸疼。我到药店买了一瓶阿司匹林，吃了两片，可是这药好像也不管用，我的头越来越疼，到了下午，我开始发烧，浑身发冷，觉得恶心，吐了两次。我赶紧去看医生，告诉他我的病情，已经吃过两种药都没用，要求他给我消炎药和打退烧针。医生给我做了检查以后告诉我："你的体温是102度，你得了流感，打针和消炎药都没有用，我给你开这种专治流感的药，你回家后还要好好多休息、多喝水，尽量不要出门把流感传染给别人"。

注 Notes

4. 把 . . . . . . 传染给 *bǎ . . . chuánrán gěi . . .* to infect . . . with . . .
   When the Chinese say "infect someone," they often will add the word 给 after 传染, followed by the person (or people) who is infected.
5. A temperature of 102 degrees Fahrenheit might be written 102°F, but it is stated as 华氏一百零二度 *huáshì yìbǎi líng èr dù* (or 一百零二华氏度). It is also acceptable to use Chinese characters for all the symbols.

   Examples of temperatures:
   100°F = 华氏一百度
   99°C = 摄氏九十九度 or 九十九摄氏度
   Example distance: 75 mph = 时速75英里 (每小时英里/公里速度)
   Example angle: 360° = 360度

3.3 Exercise 2—Vocab Grab

Review Models A and B. How can you talk about the following?

Your head hurts.

Your stomach hurts.

You are nauseous or vomited.

You have a temperature.

You have a sore throat.

You have the flu.

3.3 Exercise 3—Writing about Being Sick

Use the text builder to plan out the draft of your essay one paragraph at a time.

Paragraph 1: Describe an illness you have had. Include when it happened and your symptoms.	我病了。 我头疼。
Paragraph 2: Describe how you dealt with the illness and how long you were ill. Adapt phrases from the models. Use some of the phrases below to get started.	我去看医生 / 我去医院 / 我去睡觉 (sleep) 我吃药 我喝了很多水 / 我睡了很多觉 我病了几天 / 一个星期 / 很久 (a long time)
Paragraph 3: What can you do to prevent getting sick again or to stay as healthy as possible?	我运动得更多 (more active) /我经常锻炼 (exercise) 我比以前少吃垃圾食品 (junk food) /我吃健康的食物 (healthy food) 我吃了很多水果和蔬菜 (fruits and vegetables) 我不抽烟 (smoke) 我很少喝酒 (alcohol) 我做瑜伽 (yoga) 我减肥了(lose weight)

Writing about a Time You Were Sick

Step 1: Following the model and using your vocabulary and phrases fromabove, draft your essay one paragraph at a time.

Step 2: Review Notes 1–5 in this section and check that you haven't made any mistakes related to those notes in your essay.

Step 3: Edit and polish your essay before handing it in for feedback, assessment, or adding to your writing portfolio

3.4 五花八门的人生阅历 Various Life Experiences—我的周末 A Typical Weekend—Level B

生词与短语 Words and Phrases 3.4

开心	*kāixīn*	happy; enjoyable
大多数	*dàduōshù*	the great majority
由……组成的	*yóu . . . zǔchéngde*	to consist of . . .
独自	*dúzì*	alone; by oneself
相处	*xiāngchǔ*	spend time
玩游戏	*wán yóuxì*	play games
驾校	*jiàxiào*	driving school
教练	*jiàoliàn*	usually means "coach" for athletics, but in this context means "instructor"
料理店	*liàolǐdiàn*	(Japanese) restaurant
寿司	*shòusī*	sushi
搞笑	*gǎoxiào*	funny; hilarious
哈哈大笑	*hāhā dàxiào*	laugh heartily; burst into laughter
四川	*Sìchuān*	Sichuan Province
正宗	*zhèngzōng*	authentic
之间	*zhī jiān*	among; between
看望	*kànwàng*	visit; call on
老人家	*lǎo rén jiā*	respectful term for older people
素食	*sùshí*	vegetarian
味道	*wèidào*	taste; flavor
棒极了	*bàngjíle*	awesome; terrific
商场	*shāngchǎng*	shopping place
逛	*guàng*	window-shop; stroll around
日用品	*rìyòngpǐn*	articles for daily use
本地	*běndì*	local
幼儿园	*yòuéryuán*	kindergarten
志愿工作	*zhìyuàn gōngzuò*	volunteer work
忙碌	*mánglù*	busy; occupied

B

开心的周末

我和大多数人一样，周末的时间是由个人独自相处、与家人朋友相处组成的。平常没时间看的电视节目和书我都会利用周末的时间来看。我也会和家人朋友聊天、玩游戏、出去吃饭。

这个周六早上七点我就出门去和驾校的教练学了一个半小时的车。回家后，我看了两个小时的书。中午，我和妈妈去了一家日本料理店吃了寿司，很好吃。下午回家后，我看了韩国的搞笑节目《Running Man》，这个节目非常好玩，我看得哈哈大笑。晚上，我和两个好朋友出去吃了四川菜，非常正宗！朋友之间聊天也聊得非常开心。

星期天早上，我又去学了两个小时的车，然后去了奶奶家看望老人家。中午，我和爸爸妈妈去一家素食餐厅吃饭，味道棒极了！饭后，我和妈妈在大商场逛了逛，买了几件衣服和日用品。晚上，我为周一去本地的一家幼儿园做志愿工作做了准备。

一个忙碌但开心的周末就这样过去了！

3.4 Exercise 1—Vocab Building

1. Which of these might be part of your typical weekend? Check all that apply.

________ 看望家人	________ 去餐馆
________ 玩游戏	________ 做功课
________ 出去吃饭	________ 玩电子游戏 (play video games)
________ 动手做东西	________ 去徒步旅行 (to go hiking)
________ 去咖啡馆	________ 散步
________ 上脸书	________ 慢跑 (jogging)
________ 逛街	________ 运动
________ 做志愿工作	________ 打球
________ 看节目	________ 和朋友聊天 (to talk with friends)
________ 看电影	________ 去教堂 / 去清真寺 / 去寺庙 (go to church / mosque / temple)

2. What other activities are part of a typical weekend for you? How can you talk about them in Chinese?

注 Notes

In writing about a sequence of events in Chinese, use the following adverbs and connecting words:

- 先 *xiān* first
- 然后 *ránhòu* after that (can be used for past, present, or future actions, but only in describing a second action that logically follows a previous action)
- 以后/后 *yǐhòu/hòu* afterward (can be used for past, present, or future actions if it follows a verb; however, if 以后 is used at the beginning of a sentence or clause, it can only refer to future actions)
- 后来 *hòulái* afterward; later (only used for actions in the past and does not directly follow a verb)
- 最后 *zuìhòu* finally (can be used in any tense)

For example:

昨天是周六，我们本来打算上午先去购物中心买东西，然后去餐馆吃午饭。可是还不到十点的时候，多日不见的朋友小林来看我们，我们很高兴，大家一起动手在家里做了午饭。吃完了午饭以后，我们又聊了一下午，后来我们决定一起出去吃晚饭。和小林告别以后，我们又去超市买了东西，最后晚上11点半才回到家。

告别 *gàobié* say goodbye; part

3.4 Exercise 2—Drafting an Essay about Your Weekends

1. Grab phrases that you will need to talk about the different days of a typical weekend. Collect your phrases in the columns below.
2. Include details like times of day or how long you spend doing something.
3. Review the notes on sequencing words and adverbs and plan where to include these in your essay.

星期五晚上 **Friday evening**	星期六 **Saturday**	星期日 **Sunday**

Writing about a Typical Weekend

Step 1: Draft a paragraph for each day, using your phrases from each column in the table.

Step 2: Add a last paragraph with some general comment about your weekend. Use the following words and phrases: 忙, 快乐, 一般来说我的周末是这样度过的 (typical), 无聊 (boring), 令人兴奋的 (exciting), 好, 令人愉快的 (enjoyable)

Step 3: Exchange completed essays with someone and compare weekends. Name some similarities and differences.

3.5 娱乐和休闲活动 Pastimes—我最喜欢的体育运动 My Favorite Sports—Level A

A

我最喜欢的体育运动

我最喜欢的体育运动是棒球。我很小的时候就跟我爸爸一起看棒球比赛。我们最喜欢的棒球队是芝加哥的白袜队。每当电视上播白袜队的比赛時我们就会一起为我们的球队喊"加油"。我十二岁那年，白袜队打得越来越好，最后竟然打进了决赛！决赛那天，我和爸爸早早就坐在沙发上等着看比赛。白袜队一开始领先，但对方很快就把比分追上来了，我们都感到很紧张。每当白袜队得分，我们就激动地大喊大叫。双方打到四比四平，我们都紧张得喘不过气来。最后，白袜队的最有名的球员得分，我们赢了！白袜队为芝加哥取得了美国最好的棒球队的荣誉，我们都为白袜队感到骄傲。白袜队回到芝加哥那天，成千上万的人上街庆祝，就像过节一样！

生词与短语 Words and Phrases 3.5

棒球	*bàngqiú*	baseball
棒球队	*bàngqiúduì*	baseball team
白袜队	*Báiwàduì*	White Sox (team)
播	*bō*	broadcast
喊	*hǎn*	shout; yell
加油	*jiāyóu*	come on!; go, team!
竟然	*jìngrán*	unexpectedly; actually
打进决赛	*dǎjìn juésài*	make it into the finals
领先	*lǐngxiān*	to be leading
对方	*duìfāng*	the opponent; the other team
比分	*bǐfēn*	the score
追上来	*zhuīshànglái*	catch up
紧张	*jǐnzhāng*	nervous
得分	*défēn*	score (points or runs)
激动	*jīdòng*	excited
双方	*shuāngfāng*	both sides
……比……平	*. . . bǐ . . . píng*	tied at . . .
喘不过气来	*chuǎnbúguò qì lái*	unable to breathe
球员	*qiúyuán*	ball player
取得	*qǔdé*	gain; get
荣誉	*róngyù*	glory; honor
为……感到骄傲	*wèi . . . gǎndào jiāo-ào*	feel pride in
上街	*shàngjiē*	go out on the streets
庆祝	*qìngzhù*	celebrate

3.5 Exercise 1—Vocab Grab

1. Talking about *when* (in your life)

   What do the following example phrases mean?

   我小的时候

   我十二岁那年

   当我还在高中的时候

   五年前

   现在

2. Talking about *how often*

从来不	never	偶尔	once in a while
经常	often	常常	very often
一个月两次	two times a month	每月三次	________ times a month
每周两次	two times a week	一周五次	________ times a week
一天两次	two times a day	每天一次	________ time a day

3. How would you write the following:

when I was very young	three times a week
when I was nine years old	once a week
three years ago	once a month

3.5 Exercise 2—Planning Your Essay

Paragraph 1: Start building your short text about your favorite sport. Use the sentence builders and include phrases to talk about when and how often.

我最喜欢的体育运动是______	棒球	baseball	
我看了______	(踢 *tī*) 足球	soccer	
我打棒球______	(打) 美式足球	American football	
我的朋友打______	篮球	basketball	
	排球	volleyball	
	网球	tennis	
	高尔夫球	golf	
我喜欢______	散步	take a walk	
我不喜欢______	跑步	run	
	举重	lift weights	

Paragraph 2: Add interest to your short essay by including one of the following:

- Share what you like about your favorite sport or physical activity.
- Share with whom you do the activity and why.
- Share an interesting story or memory related to your favorite sport.

Writing about My Favorite Sport
Step 1: Put together your two paragraphs and check the words or phrases you are not sure of.
Step 2: Exchange essays with someone else and review any sections that are unclear.
Step 3: Do a final read through and make final edits before handing in your essay.

3.6 娱乐和休闲活动 Pastimes—我的爱好 My Hobbies—Level A

生词与短语 Words and Phrases 3.6 A

泰迪小熊	*tàidí xiǎoxióng*	teddy bear
一遍一遍地	*yíbiàn yíbiànde*	again and again
听课	*tīngkè*	listen to the lecture
乱	*luàn*	randomly
涂画	*tú huà*	scribble; sketch
涂满	*tú mǎn*	fill with scribbles
图画	*túhuà*	drawing; picture
并(没有)	*bìng (méiyǒu)*	actually didn't
批评	*pīpíng*	criticize
只是	*zhǐshì*	only
电子游戏	*diànzǐ yóuxì*	video games
寂寞	*jìmò*	lonely
其实	*qíshí*	actually; in fact
不再	*búzài*	no longer
而是	*ér shì*	rather
写生	*xiěshēng*	paint or sketch from nature

A

我的爱好

我从很小的时候就喜欢画画。我看到什么就想**把它画下来**。妈妈送给我的泰迪小熊、爸爸送给我的玩具火车，我都一遍一遍地画。

上小学时，上课的时候我也一边听课一边就在纸上乱涂画，连我的作业上也都涂满了我的图画，但是我的老师并没有批评我，她只是告诉我应该下课以后、做完作业以后再画画，她还送给我一本图画书。

别的小孩子周末的时候喜欢看电视、玩电子游戏、或者跟朋友们打球，可是我喜欢坐在桌前画画。我的爸爸总是对我说："儿子，天气很好，为什么不到外面去玩呢？"爸爸以为我一个人画画一定会觉得很寂寞，其实他不明白我画画的时候感到很快乐。

现在我还喜欢画画，而且越画越好。周末的时候，我还是常常画画，只是现在我不再坐在家里画画，而是常常到公园里、树林里、湖边上去写生。

3.6 Exercise 1—Reading Check

1. Describe the elementary school teacher. What role did she play?
2. How does the author describe himself compared to other children?
3. How is painting now different from painting as a child for the author?

注 Notes

1. The word *it* (它) is usually implied in Chinese, rather than being spoken or written.

   例句 **Example Sentences**

   A: Do you like that T-shirt? 你喜欢那件T恤衫吗？
   B: Yes, I like it. 我喜欢。

   A: Did you buy that book? 你买了那本书吗？
   B: Yes, I did. (Yes, I bought it.) 我买了。

   However, there are two instances when the Chinese will say and write the word *it* (它).

2. Use 它 when you refer to an animal or object and use the word *it* as the subject of the sentence, rather than name the animal or object.

   那边有一只猫。它有黑色的毛。
   Nàbiān yǒu yīzhī māo. Tā yǒu hēisède máo.
   There is a cat over there. It has black fur.

3. Use 它 when the word *it* is used in the 把 pattern.

   "我的书在哪里?" "我把它放在桌子上了。"
   "Wǒde shū zai nǎlǐ?" "Wǒ bǎ tā fàngzài zhuōzi shàng le."
   "Where is my book?" "I put it on the table."

   把它画下来 *bǎ tā huàxiàlái* draw it

3.6 Exercise 2—Vocab Grab

Practice talking about how often you do these activities and which activities you enjoy most and least.

(踢) 足球

(打) 美式足球

跑步

写生

电脑游戏 (computer games)

读书 (reading books)

做饭 (cooking food)

看电影 (watching movies)

做瑜珈 (doing yoga)

野营 (camping)

What other activities not on the list are your favorites?

3.6 娱乐和休闲活动 Pastimes—我的爱好 My Hobbies—Level B

B

野营和爬山

野营和爬山都是我最喜欢做的事情。因为我工作的时候大部分时间都是待在办公室内，所以能有机会出去探索大自然就成为我最大的享受。

跟坐在城里的办公室里的工作相比，野营和爬山让我感觉到安宁和轻松。在树林里散步，会听到小鸟唱歌、小溪里的水声。野营的晚上，常常可以看到日落时的美丽天空，然后是满天的星星。爬山的时候，更可以看到很多种动物：除了鸟和鹿以外，有时甚至能够看到黑熊！

这让我体会到我们应该更爱护大自然，因为大自然一直在保护我们。

爬山对身体健康有好处，如果你用了太多的时间在室内工作，你更应该试一试爬山运动，因为高山、江河湖海和很多美丽的野花都是在城市里找不到的。

生词与短语 Words and Phrases 3.6 B

野营	*yěyíng*	to camp
爬山	*páshān*	mountain climbing
待	*dāi*	stay; remain
内	*nèi*	inside; within
探索	*tànsuǒ*	explore
大自然	*dàzìrán*	nature
享受	*xiǎngshòu*	enjoy
跟……相比	*gēn . . . xiāngbǐ*	compare with
安宁	*ānníng*	peaceful
轻松	*qīngsōng*	lighthearted; relaxed
溪	*xī*	small stream; brook
声	*shēng*	sound
日落	*rìluò*	sunset
天空	*tiānkōng*	the sky
满天	*mǎntiān*	all over the sky
星星	*xīngxing*	stars
鹿	*lù*	deer
甚至	*shènzhì*	even; so much so that
能够	*nénggòu*	can; able to
黑熊	*hēixióng*	black bear
体会到	*tǐhuìdào*	realized
爱护	*àihù*	love; hold dear
保护	*bǎohù*	protect
对……有好处	*duì . . . yǒu hǎochù*	beneficial for
室内	*shìnèi*	indoors
江河湖海	*jiāng hé hú hǎi*	rivers and lakes and seas
野花	*yěhuā*	wildflowers

3.6 Exercise 3—Reaching Check

1. Compare the author's usual activities with the favorite free-time activities.
2. What are some of the things the author enjoys about being outdoors?
3. What questions could you ask to get to know the author and this hobby better?

3.6 Exercise 4—Planning Your Paragraphs

Use these tips and guiding questions to plan each paragraph. Which words and phrases will you need?

Paragraph 1: What are your favorite hobbies or leisure activities?
. . . . . . 都是我最喜欢做的事情

How often or for how long each time do you do this activity? Refer to 3.5 Exercise 1 on expressing *when* and *how often*.

Explain why you do this activity:
因为我在工作的时候 . . . . . . 就成为我最大的享受
因为我上大学的时候

让我感觉到 安宁 (peaceful)/ 轻松 (relaxed)/ 愉快 (happy)/ 有活力 (energetic)

Paragraph 2: Compare your hobby to what you spend the most time doing or to another activity.
跟坐在城里的办公室里的工作相比
跟与在大学学习相比

Describe more specifically what you do in pursuing your hobby.

Paragraph 3: Comment on the value, appeal, or benefits of your hobby.
. . . . . . 对身体健康有好处 (health)
. . . . . . 对你的人际关系有好处 (relationships)
. . . . . . 对你的心理健康有好处 (mental health)

Writing about Your Favorite Hobbies

Step 1: Using your notes above, draft each of your paragraphs.

Step 2: Compare your essay to 3.6 Model B. Highlight the words and phrases that you used in your essay. Check especially for the phrases that were emphasized in 3.6 Exercise 3.

Step 3: Proofread and polish your essay before submission.

3.7 娱乐和休闲活动 Pastimes—我最喜欢的电影 My Favorite Movie—Levels A and B

A

我最喜欢的电影

我最喜欢的电影是Finding Nemo。这部电影是卡通片的经典。我觉得这真是让人百看不厌的历险电影。我能背诵这部电影里的所有的台词，我的家人甚至不让我和他们一起看这部电影，因为我不断地背诵台词气得他们发疯！

我喜欢这部电影里的每一个人物，但最让我感动的是电影里表现的永恒的爱。

生词与短语 Words and Phrases 3.7 A

部	*bù*	measure word for movies
卡通片	*kǎtōngpiàn*	cartoon
经典	*jīngdiǎn*	classic
百看不厌	*bǎi kàn búyàn*	never get tired of watching
历险	*lìxiǎn*	experience adventures
背诵	*bèisòng*	recite
所有的	*suǒyǒude*	all
台词	*táicí*	actor's lines
甚至	*shènzhì*	even; so much so that
不断地	*búduànde*	unceasing
气得	*qìde*	so angry that
发疯	*fāfēng*	go crazy
人物	*rénwù*	person; figure; character (in a work of art)
感动	*gǎndòng*	be moved/touched
表现	*biǎoxiàn*	display; show
永恒	*yǒnghéng*	eternal; perpetual

注 Notes

The word 让 (*ràng*) is an excellent example of how ambiguous the Chinese language often seems compared to English. 让 can mean "to allow/let someone do something," if the action talked about is something we assume the person would want to do. For example, 我小的时候，每到周末我妈妈就会让我看电视看到很晚。(When I was little, every weekend my Mom would let me stay up late to watch TV.) 让 can mean "to make someone do something" if the action mentioned is something we assume the person would not otherwise wish to do. For example, 我小的时候我妈妈让我学钢琴。(When I was little, my mom made me learn to play the piano.) 让 can also simply mean "to have someone do something." For example, 我们的老师让我们把每一个字抄写五次。(Our teacher has us copy each new character five times.)

In Model A, the word 让 is used in yet another way. In the phrases 让人百看不厌 (makes one never tired of watching) and 让我感动 (makes me feel moved, i.e. moves me), 让 means "to make someone feel a certain way."

生词与短语 Words and Phrases 3.7 B

蜘蛛	*zhīzhū*	spider
侠	*xiá*	knight; chivalrous person
主角	*zhǔjué* (usually pronounced *zhǔjiǎo*)	leading role; protagonist
彼得	*Bǐdé*	Peter (transliteration)
普通	*pǔtōng*	ordinary; common; average
昆虫	*kūnchóng*	insect(s)
研究室	*yánjiūshì*	lab
参观	*cānguān*	visit; sightseeing
咬	*yǎo*	bite
醒来	*xǐnglái*	wake up
不可想像的	*bùkě xiǎngxiàng de*	unbelievable
发生	*fāshēng*	happen; occur
爬	*pá*	crawl; climb
射出	*shèchū*	shoot out
蜘蛛网	*zhīzhūwǎng*	spiderweb
超级能力	*chāojí nénglì*	superpower
纽约	*Niǔyuē*	New York
抓	*zhuā*	seize; arrest
并(不)	*bìng(bù)*	actually not; on the contrary
物种	*wùzhǒng*	species
渐渐地	*jiànjiànde*	gradually
仗义	*zhàngyì*	from a sense of justice

B

童年时最棒的电影

我小时候最喜欢的电影是《蜘蛛侠》。电影的主角是一个叫做彼得的普通的高中学生。有一天，彼得和他的科学课的全班同学一起到一个动物和昆虫研究室去参观。彼得在给昆虫照相时被一只蜘蛛咬了，他觉得很困，回到家就去睡觉了。可是当他醒来时，不可想像的事情发生了：他变成了一个蜘蛛侠，能和蜘蛛一样爬墙和射出蜘蛛网。从这时起，他就变成了一个具有超级能力的人，他开始帮助纽约的警察抓坏人。一开始，人们并不喜欢蜘蛛侠，因为他们觉得他跟自己是不一样的物种。但是渐渐地人们开始喜欢蜘蛛侠，因为他总是仗义助人。

3.7 Exercise 1—Reading Check

Level A

1. How is *Finding Nemo* described?
2. What does the author appreciate most about the movie?
3. Which 卡通片 is your favorite?

3.7 Exercise 2—Text Analysis

Level B

1. How does the author describe the protagonist? What types of things are mentioned?
2. According to the author, what makes the people in the story like the protagonist?
3. Compare Level A with the first part of Level B. What content can you include to enrich an essay about a favorite movie?

B

(蜘蛛侠 *continued*)

我觉得如果电影就这样结束该会是多么好啊！因为接下来的故事就是好莱坞的电影的老套：《蜘蛛侠》的另外一个主要人物就是绿恶魔，他和蜘蛛侠一样拥有超人能力，他想杀死蜘蛛侠，因为那样他就会成为世界上最强大的恶魔。蜘蛛侠因此必须要和绿恶魔作战，因为绿恶魔欺负好人。故事的最后好人终于赢了，在纽约人的帮助下，蜘蛛侠杀死了绿恶魔。

我特别喜欢这部电影是因为蜘蛛侠太帅了！我也想当蜘蛛侠，用自己的超人能力来帮助好人。第二个原因是因为蜘蛛侠的女朋友特别漂亮，哪个男孩子会不喜欢漂亮的女孩子呢？

生词与短语 Words and Phrases 3.7 B (*continued*)

结束	*jiéshù*	end; conclude
该	*gāi*	ought to (short for 应该)
接下来	*jiēxiàlái*	continuing on
好莱坞	*Hǎoláiwū*	Hollywood
老套	*lǎotào*	old and clichéd
人物	*rénwù*	person; figure; character (in a work of art)
恶魔	*èmó*	demon; devil
拥有	*yōngyǒu*	possess; have
超人	*chāorén*	superhuman
强大	*qiángdà*	powerful; formidable
因此	*yīncǐ*	therefore
作战	*zuò zhàn*	battle with
欺负	*qīfu*	bully
终于	*zhōngyú*	at last; finally
帅	*shuài*	both handsome and cool (slang)

3.7 Exercise 3—Vocab Grab

Match the Chinese to the best English equivalent.

帅 | 美丽	young | old
软弱 (ruǎnruò) | 强大	handsome | beautiful
富裕 | 穷	rich | poor
年轻人 | 老年人	weak | powerful
忠诚 (zhōngchéng)	kind
聪明	ordinary
善良	devoted; loyal
愤怒	intelligent
普通	angry

3.7 Exercise 4—Text Analysis

1. Which 超级能力 does the author talk about?
2. Which 超级能力 do you think would be most interesting?
3. How are the two characters contrasted?
4. In the last paragraph, what additional reasons does the author give for liking the movie?

注 Notes

5. 当 . . . . . . 时 (的时候) *dāng . . . shí (de shíhou)* when

例句 **Example Sentences**

当你见到他时，请把这本书还给他。
Dāng nǐ jiàndào tā shí, qǐng bǎ zhèběn shū huángěi tā.
When you see him, please return this book to him.

当她终于回到家时，全家人都欢呼起来。
Dāng tā zhōngyú huídào jiā shí, quán jiārén dōu huānhūqǐlái.
When she finally returned home, the entire family started to cheer.

3.7 Exercise 5—Planning Your Paragraphs
Use the sentence builders below to start writing. Use the tips and guiding questions to plan each paragraph. Which words and phrases will you need?

Paragraph 1: Give the name of a favorite movie and the names of the main actors (in English if you can't find their names in Chinese).
我最喜欢的电影是 . . . . . .
我最喜欢的电影演员是 . . . . . .

Paragraph 2: Describe two of the characters. Include adjectives and some of the important things that happen.
主角 . . . . . .
另外一个主要人物 . . . . . .

Paragraph 3: Comment on what you think is special or enjoyable about this move. Why would you recommend it to others?
最让我感动的是 . . . . . .
我特别喜欢这部电影是因为 . . . . . .

Writing about a Favorite Movie
Step 1: Draft each paragraph using your notes above.
Step 2: Compare your draft with Models A and B. Are there topics, words, or phrases from the models that you can adapt and add to your essay?
Step 3: Proofread and polish your essay before submitting as a class assignment.

3.8 娱乐和休闲活动Pastimes—最难忘的一次旅行 My Favorite Trip—Levels A and B

生词与短语 Words and Phrases 3.8 A

难忘	*nánwàng*	unforgettable; memorable
土耳其	*Tǔěrqí*	Turkey
伊斯坦布尔	*Yīsītǎnbùěr*	Istanbul
大巴	*dàbā*	tourist bus
卡帕多西亚	*Kǎpàduōxīyà*	Cappadocia
初夏	*chū xià*	early summer
沿途	*yántú*	along the way
野花	*yěhuā*	wildflowers
开放	*kāifàng*	come into bloom
旅店	*lǚdiàn*	small inn
提供	*tígōng*	provide; offer
传统	*chuántǒng*	tradition(al)
家常	*jiācháng*	home-style
面包	*miànbāo*	bread
奶酪	*nǎilào*	cheese (there are many synonyms in Chinese)
橄榄	*gǎnlǎn*	olives
运气	*yùnqi*	luck; fortune
闲聊	*xiánliáo*	chat
该死	*gāisǐ*	darn
蚊子	*wénzi*	mosquitoes
山谷	*shāngǔ*	mountain valley
雕刻	*diāokè*	carving
岩洞	*yándòng*	grotto
教堂	*jiàotáng*	church
偷偷地	*tōutōude*	stealthily; quietly
爬	*pá*	crawl; creep
狠狠地	*hěnhěnde*	ferociously; ruthlessly
咬	*yǎo*	bite

A

最难忘的一次旅行

我最难忘的一次旅行是我在高二的时候和我的家人一起到土耳其去。我们到了土耳其的伊斯坦布尔以后就坐旅游大巴到卡帕多西亚去。我们早上8点出发，晚上6点才到。因为那时正是初夏，沿途到处都是野花开放，非常美丽。

我们住的小旅店提供早饭，所以每天早上我们全家人一起吃传统的家常早餐：有鸡蛋、面包、奶酪、西红柿、黄瓜、橄榄等等，如果我们运气好，还会有新鲜的水果。我想在这次旅行中我最喜欢的事就是和我的家人每天一起一边吃早餐，一边闲聊。

这次旅行中我最不喜欢的事情就是那些该死的蚊子，每当我们去山谷里看那些古老的雕刻在岩洞里的教堂时，蚊子就偷偷地爬进我的衣服，狠狠地咬了我。

3.8 Exercise 1—Reading Check

1. When and where did this favorite trip happen?
2. What did the author like most about the trip?
3. What did the author like least about the trip?

B

意大利之旅

去年夏天，我和我的家人到意大利去旅行。我和我的妈妈花了很长的时间来计划这次人生的难得机会。我们全家都渴望看到罗马的圆形斗兽场和佛罗伦萨的米开朗琪罗的大卫雕像。

坐飞机到达佛罗伦萨，取了行李后，我们先来到宾馆，我们高兴地发现：这座美丽的宾馆位于一个小型广场上，旁边就是一座巴洛克风格的小教堂。

放下行李，我们便去吃我们渴望已久的第一顿正宗的意大利菜。我们在迷宫一般的狭窄的小巷里和宽广华丽的大街上穿行了很久，终于找到了一家小餐馆，其实这主要是因为站在门口的男侍者笑着用英语招呼我们进店用餐。

生词与短语 Words and Phrases 3.8 B

之	*zhī*	used in place of 的 in formal writing
难得	*nándé*	hard to come by; rare
渴望	*kěwàng*	thirst for sth.
罗马	*Luómǎ*	Rome
圆形斗兽场	*Yuánxíngdòushòuchǎng*	Colosseum
佛罗伦萨	*Fóluólúnsà*	Florence
米开朗琪罗	*Mǐkāilǎngqíluó*	Michelangelo
大卫雕像	*Dàwèi diāoxiàng*	Statue of David
到达	*dàodá*	arrive
取	*qǔ*	retrieve; pick up
宾馆	*bīn-guǎn*	guesthouse; hotel
发现	*fāxiàn*	discover
座	*zuò*	measure word for large structures such as buildings, as well as for cities
位于	*wèiyú*	be located in; be situated in
小型	*xiǎoxíng*	small-sized; small-scale
广场	*guǎngchǎng*	public square
巴洛克	*Bāluòkè*	Baroque
风格	*fēng-gé*	style
便	*biàn*	then
渴望已久	*kěwàng yǐjiǔ*	long eagerly awaited
正宗	*zhèngzōng*	authentic
迷宫	*mígōng*	labyrinth; maze
一般	*. . . yībān*	the same as; just like
狭窄	*xiázhǎi*	narrow
小巷	*xiǎoxiàng*	lane; alley
宽广	*kuānguǎng*	broad; extensive

生词与短语 Words and Phrases 3.8 B

华丽	*huálì*	magnificent
穿行	*chuānxíng*	go through
终于	*zhōngyú*	at last; finally
侍者	*shìzhě*	waiter
招呼	*zhāohu*	beckon; call; hail
用餐	*yòngcān*	have a meal

B

我当然订了比萨饼，那是我有生以来吃到的最好吃的比萨饼！比萨饼上堆满了新鲜的意大利白色奶酪和火腿，下边则是脆脆的、薄薄的饼皮。

第二天一早我们就上了旅游大巴去看托斯卡纳的风光。我们参观了几座中世纪的城堡，我们非常喜欢在这些美丽的小城堡里散步，欣赏那些古色古香的小商店。中午我们在一座葡萄酒庄里吃饭，那是有七道菜和五、六种不同的红酒的午饭！

下午我们回到佛罗伦萨，赶紧去看大卫的雕像，那真是令人惊奇的雕像，比我想象的还要巨大！

(Continues on the next page.)

生词与短语 Words and Phrases 3.8 B

比萨饼	*bǐsàbǐng*	pizza
有生以来	*yǒu shēng yǐlái*	since one's birth
堆满	*duīmǎn*	pile up
奶酪	*nǎilào*	cheese (there are many synonyms in Chinese)
火腿	*huǒtuǐ*	ham
则	*zé*	then (literary; more elegant than 就)
脆脆	*cuìcuì*	crispy
薄薄	*báobáo*	really thin
饼皮	*bǐngpí*	crust
大巴	*dàbā*	tourist bus
托斯卡纳	*Tuōsīkǎnà*	Tuscany
风光	*fēng-guāng*	scene; view
中世纪	*zhōng shìjì*	the Middle Ages
城堡	*chéngbǎo*	castle
欣赏	*xīnshǎng*	appreciate
古色古香	*gǔsègǔxiāng*	quaint; antique
葡萄酒庄	*pútáo jiǔzhuāng*	winery
道	*dào*	measure word for courses in a meal
令人惊奇	*lìng rén jīngqí*	amazing (literally, "makes people feel amazed")
巨大	*jùdà*	huge; enormous

注 Notes

1. 每当……时 (的时候)，就……
   měidāng . . . shí (de shíhou), jiù . . .
   Every time, . . . then . . .

   例句 **Example Sentences**

   每当过中国新年时，我就更加想念我的家人。
   Měidāng guò Zhōngguó xīnnián shí, wǒ jiù gèngjiā xiǎngniàn wǒde jiārén.
   Every time we celebrate the Chinese New Year, I miss my family even more.

   在美国留学的那四年里，每当我在生活上有问题时，我就会请我的美国朋友帮助我。
   Zài Měiguó liúxué de nà sìnián lǐ, měidāng wǒ zài shēnghuóshàng yǒu wèntí shí, wǒ jiù huì qǐng wǒde Měiguó péngyou bāngzhù wǒ.
   During those four years that I was studying in the U.S. as a foreign student, every time I had a problem in my life there, I'd ask my American friends to help me.

(意大利之旅 *continued*)

第三天我们坐高速火车到了罗马，从混乱的火车站来到我们的位于市中心的精品酒店，我们发现我们会有一位曾经在纽约住过好几年的意大利导游为我们开车观看罗马的景点，说实话，要不是他开车带我们在这座热闹的城市里参观，我们真会有很大的困难的。在梵蒂冈，我们看到了西斯廷礼拜堂的壁画，那实在是令人惊叹。下午我们终于看到了我们全家人向往已久的罗马斗兽场。

罗马一站是我们意大利之旅的最精彩的片段，这座美丽的城市的历史和文化让我们全家都兴奋不已。我常常拿出我们在这座城市里照的照片来看，希望有一天我们会再一次到意大利去。

生词与短语 Words and Phrases 3.8 B (*continued*)

高速	*gāosù*	high speed
混乱	*hùnluàn*	chaotic
精品	*jīngpǐn*	boutique
纽约	*Niǔyuē*	New York
导游	*dǎoyóu*	tourist guide
观看	*guānkàn*	view
景点	*jǐngdiǎn*	scenic spot; place of interest
说实话	*shuō shíhuà*	tell the truth
参观	*cānguān*	visit; sightseeing
困难	*kùnnan*	difficulty
梵蒂冈	*Fàndìgāng*	Vatican
西斯廷礼拜堂	*Xīsītíng lǐbàitáng*	Sistine Chapel
壁画	*bìhuà*	fresco; mural
实在	*shízài*	actually
令人惊叹	*lìngrén jīngtàn*	cause people to marvel
向往已久	*xiàngwǎng yǐjiǔ*	look forward to for a long time
站	*zhàn*	a stop (on a journey)
精彩	*jīngcǎi*	splendid
片段	*piànduàn*	a part; an episode
兴奋	*xīngfèn*	get excited
不已	*bùyǐ*	endlessly; incessantly
照片	*zhàopiàn*	photograph

3.8 Exercise 2—Reading

Check

1. List some of the details about the trip: when, where, and how they got there.
2. What did they eat and drink?
3. Skim the text for these phrases. What happened at these times?
   last summer
   after we arrive (in Florence)
   at noon
   in the afternoon

注 Notes

2. 要不是…… *yào búshì . . .*
If it weren't for the fact that . . .

要不是你的朋友帮助我们找到那个地方， 我们肯定会迷路了。
Yào búshì nǐde péngyou bāngzhù wǒmen zhǎodào nèige dìfang, wǒmen kěndìng huì mílù le.
If it weren't for the fact that your friend helped us find that place, we definitely would have gotten lost.

要不是我的父亲非要我学电脑，我肯定不会选电脑专业。
Yào búshì wǒde fùqin fēi yào wǒ xúe diànnǎo, wǒ kěndìng búhuì xuǎn diànnǎo zhuānyè.
If my father hadn't insisted I study computers, I certainly wouldn't have chosen computer science as my major.

3.8 Exercise 3—Planning Your Paragraphs

Not all trips are expensive and to faraway places. You can write about any trip, near or far, to big cities, local parks, a museum, or a relative's house. Use the questions and tips below to plan your paragraphs. Use the directions and questions below to collect words and phrases you can use in your essay.

Paragraph 1: Where did you go? When, for how long, and with whom? Also mention what type of transportation you took to get there: 开车去 / 坐飞机去 / 步行去 / 骑车去 / 坐火车去

Paragraph 2: Describe what you saw or did on your trip. Use time expressions to help describe the order in which things happened.

Paragraph 3: Tell a bit about the place you went or the places you stayed. Describe the food or other things that you ate, bought, or enjoyed.

Paragraph 4: Conclude by describing what you enjoyed about the trip. Was there something that you did not like about the trip?
我想在这次旅行中我最喜欢的事就是……
这次旅行中我最不喜欢的事情就是……

Writing about a Favorite Trip
Step 1: Use your notes from above to draft your essay, one paragraph at a time.
Step 2: Compare essays with someone. Which details did each person include? How did each person make the descriptions clear and interesting?
Step 3: Polish your essay before handing it in or adding it to your writing portfolio.

第四章 Narratives and Storytelling 叙事和讲故事 4

注 Notes

The general purpose of this chapter is to help students at the low-intermediate and middle-intermediate levels of proficiency write a narrative in Chinese. In addition, it can specifically prepare students to write similar narratives based on cartoon stories that are included on the Chinese AP exam and also in exercises found in many textbooks for students at the intermediate level. The AP test in particular asks students to narrate a story with a beginning, middle, and end, and one possibility for how this is presented is a cartoon with four frames.

In this chapter you will find examples of narratives based on different four-block cartoons, to demonstrate how to create such a narrative.

Please note that these narrative models represent North American situations, to aid in the narration tasks commonly assigned in Chinese-language classes. These narratives do not represent a Chinese context or the viewpoint of a person from China.

4.1 在校园的第一天 First Day On Campus—Level B

生词与短语 Words and Phrases 4.1 B

詹姆斯	*Zhānmŭsī*	James
之前	*zhīqián*	before
双层床	*shuāngcéngchuáng*	bunk bed
上铺	*shàngpù*	upper bunk
歌手	*gēshǒu*	singer
海报	*hǎibào*	poster
挂	*guà*	hang
穿过	*chuānguò*	pass through
注册	*zhùcè*	registration; register
自助	*zìzhù*	self-serve
丰富	*fēngfù*	abundant (in variety)

B

在校园的第一天

詹姆斯是大学的新生，新学期开始之前，他的爸爸开车把他送到学校，并且帮助他把行李搬到学生宿舍里去。

在他的宿舍的房间里，双层床在房间的左边，因为他睡上铺，所以他把他最喜欢的歌手的海报挂在床上面的墙上。靠墙的那张桌子是他的，桌子上面的墙上有一张世界地图。衣橱里挂着很多他和他的同屋的衣服。

搬完家以后，詹姆斯走着穿过校园到学生注册办公室去，别的很多学生也在忙着搬进宿舍。

注完册以后，詹姆斯来到学生餐厅，看到学生的自助午餐非常丰富，他高兴极了。

4.2 去购物中心买东西 Shopping at the Mall—Level B

生词与短语 Words and Phrases 4.2 B

马克	*Mǎkè*	Mark
之前	*zhīqián*	prior to; before
富裕	*fùyù*	wealthy; well-to-do
名牌	*míngpái*	brand name
尽可能	*jìn kěnéng*	as much as possible
休闲	*xiūxián*	casual
在……看来	*zài . . . kàn lái*	as . . . sees it
原价	*yuánjià*	original price
区别	*qūbié*	difference

4.2 Exercise 1—Reading Check

Read the model text and answer the questions.

1. Why does Mark need new clothes?
2. What kind of clothes does Mark prefer? And his friend?

B

去购物中心买东西

马克很快就要成为大学的新生了，他觉得在离开家之前应该去买几件新衣服，所以他跟他的朋友们一起开车来到购物中心。

马克的朋友来自一个富裕的家庭，所以他只对名牌的衣服感兴趣。

马克却只对便宜的衣服感兴趣，因为他得尽可能省钱，再说，他更喜欢休闲的衣服，所以他去看减价30%的T恤衫和牛仔裤。

在马克看来，减价30%的便宜的衣服和原价的名牌的衣服好像没有什么区别，马克不懂为什么要花很多钱买名牌。

最后，马克的朋友买了名牌衣服，马克买到了减价的T恤衫，他们都很高兴他们买到了他们想要的东西。

4.3 在餐馆吃饭 Dining in a Restaurant—Level B

4.3 Exercise 1—Reading Check

Draw a line from each picture to the part of the text that describes it.

B

在餐馆吃饭

周末的时候，四个女大学生来到一家中国餐馆吃饭，她们告诉餐馆的女带位她们一共是四个人。

虽然她们只是四个人，但是她们订了五个菜、一个汤，这是因为她们四个人当中有一位是华裔， 而且是这家餐馆的常客，她告诉她的白人朋友这家餐馆的鱼做得很好，她们一定得尝尝。

所有的菜的味道都很好，特别是那条鱼，很快就被吃光了。大家一边吃饭一边聊天，人人都很高兴。

侍者把账单拿来了，最贵的菜是那条清蒸鱼，20块钱、糖醋肉14块、芥兰炒牛肉14块、红烧牛肉8块、豆腐小白菜7块、酸辣汤4块钱。大家都觉得这家餐馆的菜又好吃又不贵。

生词与短语 Words and Phrases 4.3 B

带位	*dàiwèi*	host or hostess; maître d’
订	*dìng*	order (food in a restaurant, books from a bookstore, etc.)
当中	*dāngzhōng*	among
华裔	*huáyì*	person of Chinese heritage
尝尝	*chángchang*	taste something
味道	*wèidào*	taste; flavor
特别是	*tèbiéshì*	especially
吃光	*chī guāng*	completely eat up
侍者	*shìzhě*	server
账单	*zhàngdān*	check; bill

4.4 到野外去 Going Out in Nature—Level B

1

2

3

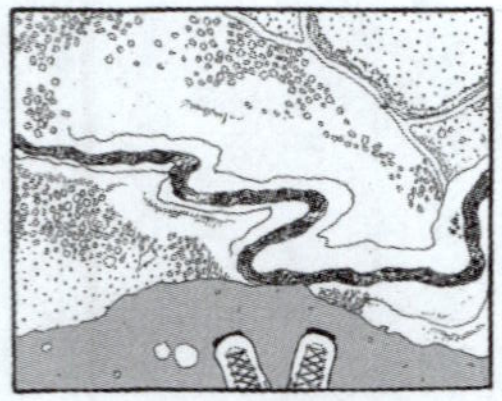
4

4.4 Exercise 1—Reading Check

Write the number of the picture in the blank that corresponds to each part of the text.

到野外去

______ 最后他们来到公园里他们最喜欢的地方——山顶上。从这里可以看到山下那条蜿蜒的小河流向前方。

______ 他们走到河边，租了一条小船以后就在河里划船玩。岸边有人在钓鱼，岸上到处都是美丽的野花和高草。

______ 周末的时候，马克、詹姆斯喜欢开车到离大学不远的一个国家公园去享受美丽的大自然。一进到公园，就会看到一条小河蜿蜒地穿过林子，在林子的后面是小山的山顶。

______ 然后他们就沿着山路爬山，游人稀少，只有鸟儿在他们的头顶上翱翔，一片平静。

生词与短语 Words and Phrases 4.4 B

野外	*yěwài*	outdoors
流	*liú*	flow
前方	*qiánfāng*	ahead
划船	*huá chuán*	row a boat
岸边	*àn biān*	shore
钓鱼	*diàoyú*	to fish
野花	*yěhuā*	wildflowers
享受	*xiǎngshòu*	enjoy
大自然	*dàzìrán*	nature
蜿蜒	*wānyán*	zigzag; meander; wind
山顶	*shāndǐng*	mountain top
沿着	*yánzhe*	along
游人	*yóu rén*	visitors (to a park)
稀少	*xīshǎo*	few; scarce
头顶	*tóudǐng*	top of the head
翱翔	*áoxiáng*	soar; hover
平静	*píngjìng*	tranquil; calm; tranquility

4.5 去国外旅行 Traveling Abroad—Level B

Below on the left are the panels, words and phrases, and model text for the first half of the next picture story. Use the pictures on the right and the remaining words and phrases to write the second half of the story in the empty box provided.

生词与短语 Words and Phrases 4.5 B

海外留学课程	*hǎiwài liúxué kèchéng*	off-campus programs
受……欢迎	*shòu . . . huānyíng*	popular with
背	*bēi*	carry on one's back
双肩包	*shuāngjiānbāo*	backpack
行李箱	*xínglixiāng*	suitcase
排队	*páiduì*	form a line; stand in line
等待	*děngdài*	wait; await
安检	*ānjiǎn*	security check (安检 is shortened from 安全检查 ānquán jiǎnchá)
课程	*kèchéng*	course (in school)
内容	*nèiróng*	content
丰富	*fēngfù*	rich; abundant
巴黎	*Bālí*	Paris
伦敦	*Lúndūn*	London
选择	*xuǎnzé*	choose; select
……之一	*zhī yī*	one of the . . .
品尝	*pǐncháng*	taste; sample
美食	*měishí*	gourmet food; fine food
比萨饼	*bǐsàbǐng*	pizza
逛街	*guàngjiē*	window-shop; stroll down the street
小玩意儿	*xiǎowányìer*	knickknacks

去国外旅行 **B**

大学的海外留学课程非常受学生欢迎，每个学期都会有很多学生参加。学生们背着双肩包、拉着行李箱在机场排队等待安检。

因为海外留学的课程内容非常丰富，学生们有机会到世界各地去旅行，有的去了巴黎，有的去了伦敦，也有的选择去了北京。

4.6 看病 Visit to the Doctor's Office—Level B

Below on the right are the panels, words and phrases, and model text for the second half of the next picture story. Write the first half of the story based on the two panels and words and phrases on the left.

生词与短语 (Useful) Words and Phrases 4.6 B

流感	*líugǎn*	flu (流感 is short for 流行性感冒 *liúxíngxìng gǎnmào*)
跟着	*gēnzhe*	follow in the wake of
醒来	*xǐnglái*	wake up
流鼻涕	*liú bítì*	have a runny nose
纸巾	*zhǐjīn*	facial tissue
诊所	*zhēnsuǒ*	clinic
至少	*zhìshǎo*	at least

生词与短语 Words and Phrases 4.6 B

终于	*zhōngyú*	at last; finally
轮到	*lúndào*	someone's turn to do sth.
量	*liáng*	measure
血压	*xuěyā*	blood pressure
打针	*dǎzhēn*	get a shot
开药	*kāiyào*	write a prescription
取药	*qǔyào*	pick up medicine

看病

看病

B

终于轮到马克了，医生给他量血压、护士给他打针。最后医生给他开了药。

马克来到药房取药。

4.7 租公寓 Renting an Apartment—Level B

4.7 Exercise 1—Reading Check

In the four boxes, sketch scenes to accompany the text. Compare your storyboard with that of a fellow student.

B

租公寓

在学生宿舍住了一年以后，斯蒂夫觉得最好搬到校外去，因为宿舍的房间太小太吵，而且也不能做饭。他上网找合适的公寓。

斯蒂夫找到了他满意的公寓，他立刻就和房东签了租房合同。

他的公寓有一个卧室、一个浴室和一个厨房。虽然公寓很小，但还是比他的宿舍房间大多了，而且房费也很合理。

公寓周围的环境也不错，楼后面就是一片林子，而且公交车站就在附近，到大学去完全不必开车，很方便。

生词与短语 Words and Phrases 4.7 B

斯蒂夫	*Sīdìfū*	Stephen
上网	*shàngwǎng*	go online
合适	*héshì*	suitable; appropriate
满意	*mǎnyì*	satisfied
签	*qiān*	to sign
合同	*hétóng*	contract
合理	*hélǐ*	reasonable; equitable
周围	*zhōuwéi*	around; surrounding
公交车站	*gōngjiāochēzhàn*	(public) bus stop

4.8 圣诞节时的家人团聚 Family Gathering at Christmas—Level B

Complete the story begun below, using the panels on the left and the accompanying words and phrases.

生词与短语 (Useful) Words and Phrases 4.8 B

切	*qiē*	cut; slice
查看	*chákàn*	look on; examine
烤箱	*kǎoxiāng*	oven
享受	*xiǎngshòu*	enjoy
喜笑颜开	*xǐ xiào yán kāi*	smiling happily from ear to ear
酒杯	*jiǔbēi*	wineglass
欢乐地	*huānlède*	happily; joyously

Useful Words for Storytelling

These words appeared in the stories in the chapter. Try to use some of them in your own version of this picture story.

之前	*zhīqián*	prior to; before
以后	*yǐhòu*	after
快	*kuài*	soon; before long
然后	*ránhòu*	then
最后	*zuìhòu*	finally; at last
终于	*zhōngyú*	finally; at last
因为	*yīnwèi*	because
所以	*suǒyǐ*	and so
也是	*yěshì*	also
虽然	*suīrán*	although
当然	*dāngrán*	of course

B

圣诞节时的家人团聚

圣诞节到了，斯蒂夫和他的家人一起来到爷爷、奶奶家，其他的亲戚也都带着孩子、拿着各种各样的礼物来了。

5 第五章 E-Mails and Letters 书写信件

5.1 与朋友通信 Communicating with a Friend—Level A

A

与朋友通信

小林：

你好！

好久不见了，不知道你最近怎么样，希望你一切都好。

我去年年底换了工作，我现在给一个非政府组织工作。我非常喜欢这份工作，常常有机会从上海到纽约去出差。下个星期我又会再去纽约，如果你有时间，不知道你愿意不愿意跟我一起吃饭，我们可以到纽约的中国城去吃一顿地道的中餐，好好聊聊。你看怎么样？

希望会很快地听到你的回音，我的手机号码还是123 5567 8900。

祝好！

于奇

6月9号

生词与短语 Words and Phrases 5.1 A

与……通信	*yǔ . . . tōngxìn*	correspond in writing with . . .
好久不见	*hǎojiǔ bújiàn*	long time no see
一切	*yíqiè*	everything; all
年底	*niándǐ*	end of the year
换	*huàn*	change; exchange
非政府组织	*fēi zhèngfǔ zǔzhī*	nongovernmental organization (NGO)
份	*fèn*	measure word for jobs
纽约	Niǔyuē	New York
出差	*chūchāi*	go on a business trip
地道	*dìdào*	genuine; authentic
聊聊	*liáoliao*	chat
回音	*huíyīn*	reply
手机号码	*shǒujī hàomǎ*	cell phone number

注 Notes

1. There is a specific formula for writing letters in Chinese that is different from other kinds of writing and from the format for letters in English. The name of the person to whom the letter is addressed (小林 in the above letter) is always followed by a colon, not by a comma as is common in English, and not indented.

Sections 5.1 through 5.5 offer models for different types of written correspondence. The Words and Phrases sections will help you understand the model texts and write your own e-mails or letters. The Notes sections can help you format, punctuate, and write appropriate e-mails or letters. To draft your own text, follow the appropriate models replacing details as needed.

注 Notes

2. Rather than begin the salutation at the beginning of the letter with *Dear*, it is usual to just write the person's name and title (e.g., Mr., Ms., Dr., Professor, President). Only when the person to whom you're writing is your sweetheart or your very closest family member, such as your mother or sibling, might you consider writing 亲爱的 (*qīn-àide* dear) in front of the person's name, as in English.
3. It is customary to write 你好 or a similar salutation right after the recipient's name. It is also customary to use an exclamation mark right after 你好. If you want to show your concern about how your friend has been, you can add a line such as 近来身体是否安康 (*Jìnlái shēntǐ shìfǒu ānkāng* Recently have you been well?). But the salutation 你好 and lines such as 近来身体是否安康 should be in separate paragraphs.
4. A common phrase to put at the end of a letter in Chinese is simply 祝好, which literally means "wish (you) well" and is the Chinese equivalent of "best wishes." Even though the phrase is only two characters, it should still be preceded by at least one blank line and then also indented by the space of two characters. It is not followed by either a comma or a period, unless the writer wishes to add an exclamation point for emphasis.
5. Before typing or signing your name on the bottom of the letter, you first need to leave at least one blank line. The general rule is to then type or sign your name at least three or four spaces back from the right margin, with the date written right below your name, rather than at the beginning of the letter. Neither your name nor the date should ever be on the left of the page at the top of the letter. In an e-mail, however, you often find that people simply type their name on the bottom left of the page as we do in English and omit the date.
6. When giving a cell phone number (eleven digits in China) no hyphens are used. The number is often written as a long string of numbers, or sometimes with blank spaces between each set. For example, the phone number that would be written in English as 123 5567-8900, in Chinese would be written as either 12355678900 or as 123 5567 8900. For landline telephone numbers, a hyphen is often added right after the area code, such as 010-66668888.

与朋友通信 Communicating with a Friend—Level B

生词与短语 Words and Phrases 5.1 B

消息	*xiāoxi*	news (informal or unofficial; news in the media is 新闻 *xīnwén*)
近况	*jìnkuàng*	current situation; recent developments
如何	*rúhé*	formal for 怎么样？
遇到	*yùdào*	run into; encounter
篮球队	*lánqiúduì*	basketball team
帅哥	*shuàigē*	handsome guy; good-looking guy
初二	*chū èr*	second year of middle school
量	*liàng*	amount; quantity
增加	*zēngjiā*	increase
改	*gǎi*	correct (make corrections); revise
作文	*zuòwén*	composition; student's essay
向……问好	*xiàng . . . wèn hǎo*	give one's regards to . . .
顺利	*shùnlì*	go well; go smoothly

B

与朋友通信

李英：

你好！

很久没有听到你的消息了，近况如何？

还记得王丽吗？昨天我在街上遇到她了，她上个月结婚了。你知道她的丈夫是谁吗？他就是我们学校的篮球队的那位1号运动员帅哥！

我今年开始教初二和初三的英语，作业量比以前增加了，而且需要花更多的时间来给学生们改作文，感觉比去年忙多了。

希望你一切都好，也希望很快就会听到你的消息，替我向你的男朋友问好。

祝一切顺利！

路华

3月6号

5.1 Exercise—Review Formatting for E-Mails or Letters

1. How do you punctuate the recipient's name at the beginning of the letter?
2. What is an appropriate salutation, and how do you punctuate or indent it?
3. How do you close a letter? How do you indent, space, punctuate, and include your name and the date?

Highlight or mark up the model texts to help you remember.

5.2 请假信 Requests to Be Excused From Class or Work—Levels A and B

生词与短语 Words and Phrases 5.2 A

请假	*qǐng jià*	ask for leave
尊敬的	*zūnjìngde*	esteemed; honored
而且	*érqiě*	moreover
特地	*tèdì*	specially
向	*xiàng*	to . . . (formal)
批准	*pīzhǔn*	permission; approval
此致	*cǐ zhì*	regards (at end of a letter)
敬礼	*jìng lǐ*	best wishes; respectfully
敬上	*jìngshàng*	respectfully submitted; respectfully yours

A

请假信

尊敬的王老师：

今天早上一起床我就觉得很不舒服，我嗓子疼、头疼、咳嗽，而且有一点儿发烧。我大概是感冒了，得去看病，所以今天我不能去上课，特地向您请假一天，请批准。

此致

敬礼

学生 刘力 敬上

11月26日

注 Notes

1. Although the term 请假信 is used here because it is a letter to someone, the term often used in mainland China is 请假条, referring in general to any written request for a leave of absence. The word 条originally referred to a brief note written on a strip of paper.
2. If you are writing a letter to someone who is older than you and in a position of authority over you, or in a higher position than you in a similar job, or when writing to someone you don't know, it is necessary to be more formal and to follow the customary rule to end the letter. First, leave at least one blank line right after stating the main purpose of the letter. Then in a new paragraph, indent two characters, and conclude with 此致 [literally, "(I) here deliver [this]," to mean "regards"]. Below that, in a new paragraph, without the two-character space, write 敬礼 (literally, "saluting [you]," to mean "respectfully"), in order to show your respect to the addressee.
3. Right after the word 学生 and before the letter writer's name, there should be a word space, as is also true before the word 敬上.

B

请假信

尊敬的张先生：

您好！

我晚上一回家，我妈妈就打来电话，告诉我我的爷爷突然因病去世了。我非常难过，因为我是我爷爷的唯一的孙子，我们的关系一直非常亲密，所以我必须去参加他的葬礼，并且帮助我的父母料理爷爷的后事。

我知道现在是我们公司最忙的季节，但是真抱歉，我得向您请假三天，恳请批准。

再次向您道歉我必须这么突然地向您请假。

此致

敬礼

王壮壮

3月15日

注 Notes

4. Right after the student's name, the characters 敬上 (which can be shortened to 上) mean not "respectfully go up" but "respectfully offer something up," that is, to present something with respect to someone in a position of authority over you, which in this case is your teacher.
5. The phrase 请批准 (please approve this) is a polite stock phrase. You're not really waiting for your teacher's permission, but you write this to show that you respect your teacher's authority in the matter.

生词与短语 Words and Phrases 5.2 B

因病	*yīn bìng*	from an illness
去世	*qùshì*	pass away; die
亲密	*qīnmì*	close; intimate
葬礼	*zànglǐ*	funeral
并且	*bìngqiě*	moreover; furthermore
料理	*liàolǐ*	arrange; take care of
后事	*hòushì*	funeral arrangements
抱歉	*bàoqiàn*	regret; feel sorry
恳请	*kěnqǐng*	earnestly request
再次	*zàicì*	once again
道歉	*dàoqiàn*	apologize

5.2 Exercise—Review Elements of a Written Excuse

1. What are the different ways you can show respect in writing an e-mail or letter?

2. What are some key differences for a written request to be excused in Chinese and in your home culture or other languages?

5.3 邀请信 Invitation to a Dinner or Date with a Friend—Level A

A

邀请信

朋友们：你们好！

下个星期五是万圣节！请你们来我家参加我和我的室友们举行的万圣节晚会。

晚会的时间是星期五晚上7点

晚会的地点是大河市13街666号

我们的房子就在橡树公园的旁边，如果你找不到就请给我发短信，我的手机号码是909 123 5567。

因为我们都不会做饭，所以我们会订几个比萨饼，我们也准备了不少的汽水。我知道这些食品和饮料都对健康没有好处，所以如果你想吃健康的食品、喝健康的饮料，恐怕你得自己带来，真抱歉。

我们也准备了好几部恐怖电影，我们有很大的平板电视，也有很多很多的影碟，所以你们想看什么我们都会有。我们的客厅很大，有三张大沙发、两张小沙发，还有两把椅子，就像一个小型的电影院。

汤姆和他的哥哥会来，杨兰和她的妹妹也会来，李明很想来，但是他说他不喜欢看暴力的电影，你们应该说服他来。

好，星期五晚上见。

许东

10.25

附：千万别把车停在路边，因为我们这条街上不许停车。你们可以把车停在我们的房子的后边。

生词与短语 Words and Phrases 5.3 A

邀请	*yāoqǐng*	invitation; invite
万圣节	*Wànshèngjié*	All Hallows' Eve (Halloween)
室友	*shìyǒu*	roommate
橡树	*xiàngshù*	oak
发短信	*fā duǎnxìn*	send a text message
比萨饼	*bǐsàbǐng*	pizza
汽水	*qìshuǐ*	soda pop
食品	*shípǐn*	foods
饮料	*yǐnliào*	beverages
恐怕	*kǒngpà*	afraid that; perhaps
抱歉	*bàoqiàn*	apologize; regret
恐怖	*kǒngbù*	scary
平板电视	*píngbǎn diànshì*	flat-screen TV
影碟	*yǐngdié*	DVD
小型	*xiǎoxíng*	small-scale; miniature
汤姆	*Tāngmǔ*	Tom
暴力	*bàolì*	violent
说服	*shuōfú*	persuade; convince
附	*fù*	P.S. (postscript)
千万	*qiānwàn*	by all means; definitely (almost always followed by 不 or 别 to mean "definitely don't . . .")

注 Notes

1. <u>对</u> . . . . . . <u>没有好处</u>　*duì . . . méiyǒu hǎochù*　doesn't benefit . . .

   例句 Example Sentences

   抽烟<u>对</u>身体健康<u>没有好处</u>。
   Chōuyān duì shēntǐ jiànkāng méiyǒu hǎochù.
   Smoking isn't beneficial to your health.

   吃太多的盐<u>对</u>身体<u>没有好处</u>。
   Chī tàiduōde yán duì shēntǐ méiyǒu hǎochù.
   Eating too much salt isn't beneficial to your health.

2. Even though it is customary to write 你好 on a separate line below the name of the addressee, when writing an informal letter or e-mail to a friend it is not uncommon to put a greeting such as 你好 on the same line with the name of the addressee.
3. In the model texts in 5.1 and 5.2, after signing the name, the date was given in the more formal way, using the characters for 月 and 日, such as 3月6日. However, in the letter in 5.3 A, we see the more common, informal way to give the date, which is to write the number of the month and of the day separated by a period, such as 1.5.
4. If you want to add something that you forgot to mention in the main body of your letter, you can leave a blank line or two under the line in which you give your name and the date. Then start a new paragraph, with or without an indentation, with the character 附 (add; attach) and a colon, followed by what you wish to add. If you just remembered there is something else you also forgot to mention, then you follow the same rule as before, except with the word 又附 (to add again).

5.3 Exercise—Formal and Informal

1. List some phrases you can use or important things to remember for more formal e-mails and letters.

2. List some things you can do or phrases to include for more informal e-mails and letters.

5.3 邀请信 Invitation to a Dinner or Date with a Friend—Level B

生词与短语 Words and Phrases 5.3 B

满	*mǎn*	complete; fully
代表	*dàibiǎo*	represent
成年	*chéngnián*	come of age; become an adult
特殊	*tèshū*	special
意义	*yìyì*	significance; meaning
为……庆祝	*wèi sb. qìngzhù*	celebrate in honor of sb.
惊喜	*jīngxǐ*	pleasant surprise
装饰	*zhuāngshì*	decorate
蛋糕	*dàngāo*	cake
关灯	*guāndēng*	turn off the lights
藏起来	*cángqǐlái*	hide
开灯	*kāidēng*	turn on the lights
大喊	*dàhǎn*	shout
等待	*děngdài*	wait; await
回音	*huíyīn*	reply
详细情况	*xiángxì qíngkuàng*	the details

注 Notes

5. Notice that lines like 你最近怎么样？希望你一切都好, in which you want to show your concern or express your good wishes, should all be in an independent line or paragraph, not connected to the main body of the letter. This makes your wishes seem more sincere rather than just a formality.

B

邀请信

大卫：你好！

你最近怎么样？希望你一切都好。

我今天给你写信是想告诉你我们应该怎样庆祝王丽的生日。下个星期六王丽就要满21岁了。21岁代表着成年的开始，所以这个生日对她来说是有特殊意义的，我们应该为她庆祝生日，给她一个惊喜。

我们的计划是请你们那天晚上8点来我们的公寓，我们会先装饰房间，准备好蛋糕和给她的礼物，然后我们就关灯、藏起来等她回家。她会在9点下课，9点30分才会到家，她一打开门，我们就会开灯、一起大喊"生日快乐！"然后唱"祝你生日快乐"，最后我们会让她切蛋糕、给她看我们送给她的礼物。

你觉得我们的计划怎么样？我会等待你的回音。下边是生日聚会的详细情况：

时间：下星期六晚上8点

地点：绿田市蓝天街1号306公寓

希望下个星期六会见到你！

李小红

5.8

5.4 致歉函 Declining a Dinner Invitation—Level B

生词与短语 Words and Phrases 5.4 A

致歉	*zhì qiàn*	apologize; express regret
函	*hán*	formal for 信
盛情	*shèngqíng*	great kindness or hospitality
夫人	*fūrén*	wife (very formal)
晚宴	*wǎnyàn*	banquet
荣幸	*róngxìng*	be honored
受邀	*shòuyāo*	receive an invitation; be invited
前往	*qiánwǎng*	proceed to; go to
府上	*fǔshàng*	your home (formal)
做寿	*zuòshòu*	celebrate the birthday of an older person
不巧	*bùqiǎo*	unfortunately
妻子	*qīzi*	wife (formal legal term)
届时	*jiè shí*	at that time
欧洲	*Ōuzhōu*	Europe
错失	*cuòshī*	miss (a chance)
相聚	*xiāngjù*	gather together
歉意	*qiànyì*	regret; apology
望	*wàng*	hope (short for 希望)
见谅	*jiànliàng*	forgive me
敬启	*jìngqǐ*	respectfully

注 Notes

Between the name of the writer 高泰飞 and the closing phrase 敬启, there should be a blank space, to separate your expression of respect from your name.

B

致歉函

林汉中先生：

感谢盛情邀请我们参加您和夫人的生日晚宴，我们很荣幸能受邀前往府上为您做寿，十分不巧的是我和妻子届时将前往欧洲旅游，因此会错失这次与您相聚的机会，特地写信表示歉意，还望见谅。

此致

敬礼！

高泰飞 敬启

10月18日

5.4 Exercise—Using the Models for Correspondence

1. Choose the model and words and phrases that most closely align with your purpose or topic.
2. Determine the appropriate level of formality. Review the changes recommended for formal or informal correspondence and integrate the right changes.
3. Check the formatting, including when to indent and add a line.
4. Review how to punctuate (periods, commas, exclamation points, or colons).
5. Check Chapter 5 for phrases that are often used in common types of correspondence.

5.5 信件结尾时常用的习语 Commonly Used Phrases to End Letters

注 Notes

How you end a letter very much depends on your relationship to the person to whom you are writing. As in English, consider if the person is a friend, a colleague, your boss, someone much older than you, or a total stranger. Here are some common ways to end a letter."

祝好 *zhù hǎo* wishing (you) well

This is the simplest and most generic way to wish someone well, mostly used for friends, colleagues, and casual acquaintances of a similar age.

祝安好 *zhù ān hǎo* wishing (you) to be safe and sound

This should be used when writing to someone who is older than you.

此致敬礼 *cǐ zhì jìng lǐ* here I wish to extend salutations (to you).

This is used mainly for someone who is above you, both in age and social position, or for someone you don't know. It is a much more formal way to end a letter. It is also most commonly used to end a letter to a casual acquaintance to show respect.

祝新婚快乐 *zhù xīnhūn kuàilè* wishing (you, the newlyweds) happiness

祝幸福美满 *zhù xìngfú měimǎn* wishing (you) happiness and perfect conjugal happiness

To an English-speaking person, it may seem strange to wish someone perfect conjugal happiness, but this is a typical phrase to use for newly married or any married people in China.

祝万事如意 *zhù wànshì rúyì* wishing (you) will have all you hope for.

祝安康 *zhù ānkāng* wishing you good health

The character安 as in平安 peace; 康as in健康 health. Therefore, these two characters combined mean "wishing you the best of health."

恭祝安康 *gōngzhù ānkāng* respectfully wishing (you) the best of health

This is a more formal way to say the same thing as 祝安康. It should be used if you are writing to someone above you in both age and in a position of greater authority.

祝你们全家健康平安

zhù nǐmen quánjiā jiànkāng píng-ān wishing your whole family good health and peace

This is a modern, vernacular way to express this sentiment.

祝阖府安康 *zhù héfǔ ānkāng* wishing your whole household safe and sound

This phrasing employs more classical language.

祝秋安 *zhù qiū ān* wishing for your safety and health in autumn

You also can wish someone well in the other seasons, so 祝春安, 夏安, and 冬安 are all possible.

5.6 祝贺信 Congratulations—Level B

陈喜：你好！

我刚刚听说你得到了那个在联合国工作的机会，祝贺你！我真为你高兴，住在纽约，又有机会到全世界去出差，多难得啊，真羡慕你！

我也有好消息告诉你，我已经搬回了华盛顿，在乔治城大学工作。现在我们住得比以前近多了，欢迎你常来华盛顿玩，我有时间也会常去纽约看你。

给我打电话吧，我的电话号码还是909 123 4557。

祝你一切顺利！

李文

9.3

生词与短语 Words and Phrases 5.6

祝贺	*zhùhè*	congratulate
得到	*dédào*	get; obtain
联合国	*Liánhéguò*	United Nations
为 . . . . . . 高兴	*wèi . . . gāoxìng*	be happy for
纽约	*Niǔyuē*	New York
难得	*nándé*	hard to come by; rare
羡慕	*xiànmù*	admire; envy
搬回	*bānhuí*	move back to
乔治城	*Qiáozhìchéng*	Georgetown

5.6 Exercise—Analyzing the Model Text

1. Highlight or mark up elements of the model as reminders about proper indentation, formatting, and punctuation.
2. Does this note seem formal or informal? Which things could you change to make it more formal or more informal? See also the Notes sections in Chapter 4.

3. Underline key phrases in the model that you could easily use or adapt when writing your own note of congratulations.

5.7 感谢信 Thank-Yous—Level B

生词与短语 Words and Phrases 5.7

接到	*jiēdào*	receive
考进	*kǎojìn*	gain entry by passing an exam; be admitted to (a college, etc.)
音乐学院	*yīnyuè xuéyuàn*	music conservatory
完全	*wánquán*	completely; entirely
这……来	*zhè . . . lái*	for the last . . . (amount of time)
在……教导下	*zài . . . jiàodǎo xià*	under the guidance of
钢琴	*gāngqín*	piano
演奏	*yǎnzòu*	perform
技巧	*jìqiǎo*	technique; skill
理解	*lǐjiě*	understand; comprehend
经济情况	*jīngjì qíngkuàng*	financial situation
免费	*miǎnfèi*	free of charge
琴	*qín*	string instrument
真正	*zhēnzhèng*	genuine; true; real
少有	*shǎo yǒu*	rare
慷慨	*kāngkǎi*	generous
善良	*shànliáng*	kindhearted
外甥女	*wàishengnǚ*	sister's daughter; niece
提出	*tíchū*	put forward; raise

文英：

你好！

我刚刚接到我姐姐的来信，她告诉我，她的女儿能考进音乐学院，完全是因为你的帮助，因为这三年来在你的教导下，她的钢琴演奏技巧大大地提高，对音乐的理解也越来越高，姐姐的经济情况很不好，可是你一直免费地教她的女儿学琴。

这让我非常感动，你是一个真正的朋友，一个少有的慷慨的人，一个善良的人，当然，你也是一个非常好的老师。

感谢你对我的姐姐和我的外甥女的帮助，如果我能为你做一点什么，请千万别不好意思提出。

再次感谢你！

你的朋友 青静

5月5号

注 Notes

It is customary to indicate your relationship with the recipient of the letter before you type or sign your name at the end of a letter. For example, if you are writing to your parents, then you might close the letter with something like 儿 明东 (Your son, Ming Dong), or 女儿 丽丽 (Your daughter, Li Li), with a space between the character 儿 and the name of the writer. In this case, 你的朋友 is added before the letter writer's name, to honor the fact that the letter writer is the recipient's friend.

5.8 吊唁/慰问信 Condolences—Level B

安萍：

惊悉令尊不幸遽然病逝，震惊之外，不胜悲痛。上个月在你家聚会的时候老人家好像还很硬朗呀。

我知道这么突然地失去父亲是非常让人震惊的事情，也是很难让人接受的事情，希望你能节哀顺变，你只能安慰自己，你的父亲没有像很多别的老人那样，躺在病床上受到很久的病痛折磨。

我知道此刻你的心情一定很难过，有什么需要我帮忙的，千万别客气。

祝

安康！

月明

11月1号

注 Notes

The last lines of a letter when you wish someone well in a more formal way, with expressions such as 安康 or 安好, are treated as a new paragraph. Therefore, you need to leave a space of at least one blank line before writing the character 祝, indented by the space of two characters rather than on the same line. The only exception is when you end the letter with the phrase 祝好, which is always written with the two characters on the same line.

生词与短语 Words and Phrases 5.8

吊唁	*diàoyàn*	condolences; offer condolence
慰问	*wèiwèn*	express sympathy and send regards
惊悉	*jīngxī*	be shocked to learn
令尊	*lìngzūn*	your esteemed father
不幸	*búxìng*	unfortunately
遽然	*jùrán*	suddenly; abruptly (formal)
病逝	*bìngshì*	die of illness
震惊	*zhènjīng*	shock
之外	*zhī wài*	besides
不胜	*búshèng*	unbearable
悲痛	*bēitòng*	grief; sorrow
聚会	*jùhuì*	party
硬朗	*yìnglang*	hale and hearty
突然	*tūrán*	suddenly; unexpectedly
失去	*shīqù*	lose
接受	*jiēshòu*	accept
节哀顺变	*jié āi shùn biàn*	restrain grief and accept the loss (often said to the bereaved)
安慰	*ānwèi*	comfort; console
病床	*bìng chuáng*	sickbed; hospital bed
受到……折磨	*shòudào . . . zhémo*	be tormented
此刻	*cǐkè*	at this time
心情	*xīnqíng*	frame of mind; mood
千万(别)	*qiānwàn (bié)*	by all means (don't); definitely (don't)

5.9 圣诞节祝贺卡或祝贺信 Christmas Greeting Card or Letter—Level B

明远好友：

值此佳节，祝你们全家圣诞快乐，并在新的一年里健康快乐平安！

老友 力民

2021. 12. 22

生词与短语 Words and Phrases 5.9

祝贺	*zhùhè*	congratulate
卡	*kǎ*	card
好友	*hǎo yǒu*	good friend
值此	*zhí cǐ*	upon this
佳节	*jiā jié*	happy holiday time
全家	*quánjiā*	the whole family
并	*bìng*	moreover (short for 并且)
平安	*píng-ān*	safe and sound

5.10—新年祝贺卡或祝贺信 New Year's Greeting—Level A

陈晨好友：

值此佳节，祝愿你在新的一年一帆风顺，心想事成！

明兰

12. 28

生词与短语 Words and Phrases 5.10 A

祝愿	*zhùyuàn*	wish
一帆风顺	*yì fān fēng shùn*	smooth sailing
心想事成	*xīn xiǎng shì chéng*	have one's wishes come true

5.10—祝贺新年 New Year's Greeting—Level B

尊敬的王老师：

值此新年来临之际，谨向您致以节日的问候和最诚挚的祝福，并感谢您一年来对我的辛勤培育。

恭祝您新年快乐，万事如意！

学生 周晴 上

2021年12月25日

生词与短语 Words and Phrases 5.10 B

来临之际	*lái lín zhī jì*	on the occasion of
谨	*jǐn*	sincerely
致	*zhì*	send; extend
问候	*wènhòu*	greetings; regards
诚挚	*chéngzhì*	sincere; cordial
祝福	*zhùfú*	blessings; warm wishes
辛勤培育	*xīnqín péiyù*	diligent nurture
恭祝	*gōngzhù*	respectfully wish
万事如意	*wànshì rúyì*	wishing you all you hope for

注 Notes

It may seem that the phrase 恭喜发财 *(gōngxǐ fācái)*, "May you be happy and prosperous," is the most commonly used Chinese phrase for New Year's greetings. In fact, it is mainly used among Chinese people in Hong Kong and by more business-oriented Chinese people in the United States, particularly among the Cantonese-speaking population.

Although nobody would wish to not be prosperous, it is quite inappropriate to use this phrase with people whose life and work have nothing to do with business. For example, a public office employee or a salaried teacher can't 发财 (literally, become wealthy) year after year! In fact, it is seen as rather offensive because for most educated Chinese it connotes materialism.

注 Notes

There are a great number of standard phrases that the Chinese have used from ancient times for New Years' greetings, many of which are still widely used today. We generally don't recommend that you use them too liberally.

That's because these phrases, just like ones that appear in greeting cards in English, often seem like empty platitudes. Only under certain circumstances, such as when sending greetings to business associates, should you use them, because to businesspeople these greetings are commonplace and there is less expectation of creativity or individuality in this context.

Read through the following list of common courtesy phrases. As you can see, many of these phrases convey a wish for the other person to be prosperous.

5.11 新年时常用的问候语 Common Courtesy Phrases Used at Chinese New Year

恭喜发财	*gōngxǐ fācái*	wishing you happiness and prosperity
大吉大利	*dàjí dàlì*	wishing you good fortune and great profit
年年有余	*niánnián yǒu yú*	wishing you abundance every year
年年高升	*niánnián gāoshēng*	may you be promoted every year
财源广进	*cáiyuán guǎngjìn*	may your financial resources ever grow
吉祥如意	*jíxiáng rúyì*	may you have good fortune and all you wish for
万事如意	*wànshì rúyì*	may all your wishes come true
岁岁平安	*suìsuì píng-ān*	may you have peace every year
喜气洋洋	*xǐqì yángyáng*	wishing you great joy

The following three model texts are for written correspondence associated with weddings.

5.12, 5.13, and 5.14 婚礼—For Weddings

5.12 婚礼请柬—Wedding Invitation—Level B

______ 先生/太太/小姐　台启

本人(your name)谨订于2021年5月15日（星期日）（上/下）午(number of the hour)时与（name of fiancé/fiancée)在(name of hotel) 酒店(floor number)层(name of the hall)厅举行结婚典礼，敬备喜筵，恭请光临。

(your name)敬邀

生词与短语 Words and Phrases 5.12

婚礼	*hūnlǐ*	wedding; wedding ceremony
请柬	*qǐngjiǎn*	invitation card (formal)
台启	*táiqǐ*	for your kind attention
本人	*běnrén*	I (formal), myself
谨订	*jǐn dìng*	have solemnly arranged
于	*yú*	on; at; in
层	*céng*	story; floor (of a building)
厅	*tīng*	hall (for special events)
举行	*jǔxíng*	hold (a ceremony, etc.)
典礼	*diǎnlǐ*	ceremony; celebration
敬备	*jìng bèi*	have respectfully prepared; humbly offer
喜筵	*xǐyán*	wedding banquet
恭请	*gōng qǐng*	respectfully invite
光临	*guānglín*	your honorable presence
敬邀	*jìng yāo*	respectfully request or invite

注 Notes

1. There are numerous ways to write a wedding invitation in Chinese. The layout as well as the character of the language used in a wedding invitation show that formal written language and classical phrases still heavily influence wedding invitations, especially in Hong Kong and Taiwan. But to most young people in mainland China, many of these rules and the use of classical Chinese are deemed too old-fashioned and inflexible, and seem lacking in individuality. Therefore, our model is in much simpler form and in much plainer vernacular language, as is commonly used in mainland China.

5.13 接受婚礼请柬的答复信— Accepting a Wedding Invitation—Level B

秋生、雨英二位好友：

刚刚接到你们的婚礼请柬，你们自大学以来便相恋多年，却因工作而两地分居，现终于将结束爱情长跑，喜结良缘，真心为你们高兴。我当然一定会去参加你们的喜庆好事。

祝愿你们天长地久，永结同心！

友 天青

生词与短语 Words and Phrases 5.13

接受	*jiēshòu*	accept
答复	*dáfù*	reply (to a letter)
自 . . . . . . 以来	*zì . . . yǐlái*	from (such and such at time) . . . on; ever since
便	*biàn*	formal for 就 (then)
相恋	*xiāngliàn*	love each other
因	*yīn*	short for 因为
两地分居	*liǎngdì fēnjū*	to live apart in two different places
现	*xiàn*	short for 现在
终于	*zhōngyú*	at last; finally
结束	*jiéshù*	conclude; finish
爱情	*àiqíng*	(romantic) love
长跑	*chángpǎo*	long-distance race; marathon
喜结良缘	*xǐ jié liáng yuán*	happily join in marriage
真心	*zhēnxīn*	wholehearted(ly); sincere(ly)
喜庆	*xǐqìng*	happy event; celebration
祝愿	*zhùyuàn*	wish
天长地久	*tiān cháng dì jiǔ*	last as long as heaven and earth; everlasting
永结同心	*yǒng jié tóng xīn*	forever tie these hearts together as one

注 Notes

2. As we have mentioned before, it is customary to indicate your relationship with a letter's recipient before you type or sign your name at the end of the letter. For example, if you are writing to your parents, then you might close the letter with something like 儿 明东 (Your son, Ming Dong), or 女儿 丽丽 (Your daughter, Li Li), with a blank space between the character 儿 and your name. In Model 5.6, 你的朋友 is shortened into 友, to indicate that you are honoring the fact that you are this person's friend.

5.14 结婚礼物致谢函/感谢礼物函—Thank-You for Wedding Gift—Level B

天华：

我和国平都十分高兴你能来参加我们的婚礼，我们也感谢你送给我们的新颖礼物，人人都说这件礼物又别致又新奇，真可以说是人见人爱！我和国平在此表示衷心的感谢。

祝一切顺利！

友 影云

2021年6月7号

生词与短语 Words and Phrases 5.14

致谢	*zhì xiè*	express one's thanks or gratitude
十分	*shífēn*	fully; utterly; completely
新颖	*xīnyǐng*	new and original; novel
别致	*biézhì*	unique
新奇	*xīnqí*	novel; new
人见人爱	*rén jiàn rén ài*	loved by all
在此	*zài cǐ*	hereupon; here
表示	*biǎoshì*	express; show
衷心的	*zhōngxīnde*	wholehearted; heartfelt